Street Food Vending in Urban Assam

Street Food Vending in Urban Assam:

An Anthropological Appraisal

Mini Bhattacharyya Thakur

GYAN

ISBN : 978-81-212-1989-1

Published, 2022

Published by

Gyan Publishing House
5, Ansari Road
Daryaganj, New Delhi-110002
Phone: 011-47034999, 9811692060
www.gyanbooks.com
E-mail: books@gyanbooks.com

Printed at: G. Print Process, Delhi.

To my children
Rishav
And
Sanghamitra
who continue to inspire me

Contents

Preface

Street food is a type of prepared food sold on the streets and other public places from pushcarts, balance poles or temporary sheds. This work primarily records and examines the activity of street food vending in Guwahati city, the capital of Assam, by unfolding stories of life of street vendors and consumers mired in a maze of culinary practices defying norms of traditionalism, caste and commensality.

While this work began as an academic exercise, it promises applied value by giving insight into the operation of street food vending, a key component of the unorganized economy of the Indian cities. Fieldwork for this study took place from 1991 to 1993 which was followed by a survey led by the author which was conducted in 2009. This survey covered a total of 1053 street food vendors with the aim of understanding their knowledge, attitude and practices about food safety and hygiene issues. In 2019, a follow-up survey was undertaken to check if there have been any significant changes in street vending in Guwahati and to understand the variety of viewpoints on the Street Vendors Act of 2014. Though a few changes seem to have taken place since the completion of initial fieldwork as overall issues and problems of food vendors have remained the same, some of the findings from the surveys of 2009 and 2019 have been incorporated here.

This work was undertaken under the supervision of late Professor A.C. Bhagabati, former Vice-Chancellor of Rajiv Gandhi University. His erudition and scholarship have been a great source of inspiration to me.

Throughout the course of my work, I have had the opportunity to discuss the material with a number of persons. Their suggestions and opinions have helped me a great deal. I am thankful to Professor Irene Tinker, Department of City and Regional Planning, University of California, Berkeley; late Professor Md. Taher, retired Professor in Geography, Gauhati University; Mr. Atulananda Goswami, litterateur; and late Professor B.M. Das, Professor in Anthropology for their constant help and inspiration.

My sincere thanks go to Professors A.K. Bhagabati of the Department of Geography and D.C. Goswami of Department of Environmental Science, Gauhati University, for their help and cooperation. I am thankful to Dr.Bapukan Choudhury and all my colleagues, former and present, in the Department of Anthropology, Gauhati University, for their kind support.

I am grateful to Professor Sarit K Choudhuri, Rajiv Gandhi University, Arunachal Pradesh and Mr.Sudhir Srivastava of Indira Gandhi Rashtriya Manav Sangrahalaya, Bhopal, for their kind initiative in helping me get the book ready for publication.

I am indebted to a great extent to the street food vendors of Guwahati, the Municipal and the Health Authorities, without whose help and cooperation the study would not have been possible.

Last but not the least, my sincere thanks are reserved for my family- my husband, Mr. Diganta Thakur and all my family members, especially my parents, parents-in-law and my children, Rishav and Sanghamitra, whose immense patience and help in all directions saw me through.

While I am indebted to all the persons who have helped me in numerous ways, during fieldwork and at the time of preparation of this work, I take sole responsibility for any errors of omission and commission that might have remained in this work despite my best efforts.

Guwahati **Mini Bhattacharyya Thakur**

30th January 2020

List of Tables

List of Figures

List of Plates

Chapter One

Introduction

The growth of urban population has stimulated a rise in the number of street food vendors in many cities throughout the world, including Guwahati – the fast growing capital city of Assam. The presence of a floating population arriving daily in cities from rural areas as well as the movement of the urban population for work, study, shopping and for many other essential activities has created a need for many to eat a meal outside their homes.

Eating of ready to eat cooked food on the streets has been in practice since the dawn of civilization around ten thousand years ago. The ancient Greeks described the Egyptian custom, traditional in the port of Alexandria and subsequently adopted throughout Greece, of frying fish and selling it in the street. From Greece, the custom spread to the Roman world, enriched and transformed into numerous variations. In the excavations at Herculaneum and Pompei, the well-preserved remains of the "thermopolia" (a Greek term meaning a place where hot food is sold) can be seen, which many consider a forerunner of today's food stalls (www.streetfoody.it/en/street-food-the-story).

Cities are the engines of growth which drives in hundreds and thousands of workers, craftsmen, informal service providers to it. These are the people who provide daily necessities and services at an affordable price for the urban populace. The accelerated rate of growth of population in developing countries has resulted in large scale migration of people to cities and towns. This migration of rural poor to urban areas in search of work and livelihood reflects the spill-over of rural poverty (Tripathy and Das 1991:2). Economic development has failed to generate adequate employment and income opportunities in the formal sector. Under these conditions, the surplus labour force has no option but to find their own employment and source of income. The unskilled and semi-skilled rural migrants to metropolitan cities seek jobs in the informal sector of the urban economy, as construction workers, domestic servants, street food vendors, peddlers, hawkers, cycle and auto mechanics, junk collectors, basket weavers, barbers, cycle rickshaw pullers and shack shop and tea stall keepers. All these are an essential part of the urban economy. These services and activities cater to the needs of people belonging to different socio-economic strata in the towns and cities. The emergence of this 'new' category of activities involving persons engaged in a variety, of productive activities is now called the informal sector. The coexistence of two sectors, the formal and the informal, shows structural dualism in urban economy in terms of size, mode of production, technology, productivity and labour market which has assumed special importance because of the belief that economic development based on the Formal sector alone is not the most desirable way of development. A development strategy which combines or emphasizes the growth of small mid informal organization may produce quick and equitable development.

For many years, the urban street food trade was dismissed as insignificant economic activity by development economists. The marxists and liberal economists considered street food and other microenterprises as remnants of earlier economic systems which would eventually disappear as development proceeded. Despite these theoretical predictions, the vendors have not disappeared, but "have increased in variety and numbers as rural migrants flood the cities of the developing world" (Tinker 1994:4). Further, according to both the perspectives, the informal sector was expected to disappear in the wake of modernization. Both these schools of thought were forced to reinterpret theories so as to explain these economic activities. However, even after the informal sector was recognized, the tiny enterprises like street food were largely excluded from ILO research and national counting, because as single-person and family activities they were judged as too small to grow and employ others. Nevertheless, street food vending has become an integral part of urban life.

How integral are the contributions of street food vendors is highlighted in the writings of Roever and Skinner(2016) "Street vendors' contributions to urban life go beyond their own self employment". They generate demand for services provided by other informal workers and also generate demand for services provided by formal sector public and private actors, including transportation, and formal shops and suppliers from whom they source their goods. Endorsing the importance of street vending, the Supreme Court of India has said that street vendors *"considerably add to the comfort and convenience of the general public, by making available ordinary articles of everyday use for a comparatively lesser price"* (http://indiankanoon.org/doc/1767433/.)

Studies from different parts of the world also highlights the role played by informal food vendors in urban food security. The African Food Security Urban Network (AFSUN http://www.afsun.org.) for example, found that 70 per cent of households surveyed across 11 sub-Saharan African cities obtained their food from informal sources, with 59 per cent of households reporting that they patronized informal food outlets once a week or more. Further, the more food insecure the household, the more likely it is to rely on informal food sources. Steyn et al (2013) reviewed 23 studies conducted predominantly in sub-Saharan Africa similarly found that the daily energy intake from street foods in adults ranged from 13 to 50 per cent, and in several cities' street foods contributed around half of daily protein intake.

In India many people, young and old, men and women, today buy and eat commercially cooked food obtained from out-of-home sources. In the olden days, particularly for the Hindus, cooking and eating were confined to the domestic hearth - an area of high purity, even sanctity (Khare 1976). Commensality between members of different castes and communities were also restricted. Hence, partaking of cooked food outside home (where the social background and the caste of the cook are unknown) meant breaking of social norms which called for expiation rites. However, with progressive urbanization and industrialization, ritual restrictions on handling of cooked food and feeding people across caste and community lines have largely disappeared (Khare 1976a:255). This has resulted in change in culinary ethics and adoption of a new ethos wherein different types of food which are secular and not confined to the domestic hearth have come to be accepted. As Khare notes, the relaxation of caste restrictions on cooked food has become a necessity and eating out is increasingly becoming popular as a "... non- sacred, social art, activity and entertainment" (*ibid*).

INFORMAL SECTOR AND STREET FOOD VENDING

Studies carried out in the early 1970s by International Labour Office (ILO) on employment in metropolitan cities of developing countries led to a new concept which aroused a great deal of controversy: the concept of informal sector (IFS) as against the formal sector (FS), which constitute the urban economy of the Third-World countries (ILO 1972).

The accelerated rate of growth of population in developing countries has resulted in large scale migration of people to cities and towns. This migration of rural poor to urban areas in search of work and livelihood reflects the spill-over of rural poverty (Tripathy and Das 1991:2). Economic development had failed to generate adequate employment and income opportunities in the formal sector. Under these conditions, the surplus labour force has no option but to find their own employment and source of income. The unskilled and semi-skilled rural migrants to metropolitan cities seek jobs in the informal sector of the urban economy, as construction workers, domestic servants, street food vendors, peddlers, hawkers, cycle and auto mechanics, junk collectors, basket weavers, barbers, cycle rickshaw pullers and shack shop and tea stall keepers. All these are an essential part of the urban economy. These services and activities cater to the needs of people belonging to different socio-economic strata in the towns and cities. The emergence of this new category of activities involving persons engaged in a variety, of productive activities is now called the informal sector. The coexistence of two sectors, the formal and the informal, shows structural dualism in urban economy in terms of size, mode of production, technology, productivity and labour market which has assumed special importance because of the belief that economic development based on the Formal sector alone is not the most desirable way of development. A development strategy which combines or emphasizes the growth of small and informal organization may produce quick and equitable development.

Following this trend of dualism theory in urban sector, the ILO-UNDP Employment Mission to Kenya mentioned the following characteristics of the informal sector (Romatet 1983). These are:

(i) Ease of entry of new enterprises.
(ii) Family ownership.
(iii) Small size of operation.
(iv) Unregulated and competitive market.
(v) Labour Intensive technology.
(vi) Informally acquired skill through an on-the-job training.
(vii) No state support.
(viii) Deplorable working conditions and low wages.

Santos (*ibid.*, p. 2115) enlarged upon the ILO approach and added the following characteristics:

(i) There is potential for innovation.
(ii) Though employment is insecure and the number of people employed by each unit is small, yet as there are numerous small-scale units, the total number of employees are quite substantial.

(iii) Activities are based on cash transactions or on direct and personal credit.

(iv) Capital accumulation and reinvestment is low.

(v) Numerous middlemen operate between the initial supplier and the final buyer.

(vi) Exchanges are made in small quantities as investors are limited and working capital is low.

(vii) In most cases, units do not keep regular accounts.

(viii) For many years, the urban street food trade was dismissed as insignificant economic activity by development economists. The Marxists and liberal economists considered street food and other microenterprises as remnants of earlier economic systems which would eventually disappear as development proceeded. Despite these theoretical predictions, the vendors have not disappeared, but "have increased in variety and number as rural migrants flood the cities of the developing world" (Tinker 1994:4). Further, according to both the perspectives, the informal sector was expected to disappear in the wake of modernization. Both these schools of thought were forced to reinterpret theories so as to explain these economic activities. However, even after the informal sector was recognized, the tiny enterprises like street food were largely excluded from ILO research and national counting, because as single-person and family activities they were judged as too small to grow and employ others. Nevertheless, street food vending has become an integral part of urban life.

Study of food and food habits are of great relevance to economists, geographer and anthropologists. In the subject of Anthropology, during the Nineteenth century, interest on the study of food centered around taboo, totemism and sacrifice. One of the prominent figures who contributed to this field was Sir James Frazer who wrote an article on taboo and totemism for the ninth edition of Encyclopaedia Britannica. Ernest Crawley (1927) studied food as having linkage to religious aspects of sexual relations. Another favourite topic was the relation between offerings of food to the supernatural and aspects of social organization, highlighted in the well known study by Robertson Smith (1889). Radcliffe-Brown's (1948) study of the Andaman Islanders closely followed the approach of Robertson Smith. According to Radcliffe- Brown, the Andaman Islanders' most important activity is procuring food and it is around food that "the social sentiments are most frequently called into action" (*ibid.*, p. 227).

Bronislaw Malinowski was more concerned with the process of production than with symbolism. In the introduction to Audrey Richards' first essay (1932) entitled *Hunger and Work in a Savage Tribe*, Malinowski described the book as 'the first collection of facts on the cultural aspects of food and eating' (p. ix), and as laying 'the foundations for a sociological theory of nutrition' (p. x). Audrey Richards in her later book (1939:405) discussed the symbolism of cooked food in which food transaction is an indicator of social relations. Throughout her work, there is an insistence on the 'sociological aspects' of diet and the 'cultural determinants of food and feeding'. Based on the study of nutrition in Africa, Meyer and Sonia Fortes' article entitled 'Food in the Domestic Economy of the Tallensi' (1936) dealt with aspects of production and consumption at the domestic level.

The outbreak of World War II saw a cooperation between different disciplines in food related studies, leading to more practical oriented studies. The establishment of the Committee on Food Habits in United States resulted in a valuable study by Carl Guthe and Margaret Mead (1945). This work is valued for its practical applicability. Sociological aspects of nutrition in daily life and post war nutrition studies were some of the important areas of research by nutritionists and social thinkers.

In the 1960s and 1970s, the analysis of cooking has been primarily associated with the name of Claude Levi-Strauss. His focus of study is very different from that of the earlier thinkers. He attempted to study the 'deep structures' of the human mind to analyze social action. His specific theoretical interest in the subject of cooking was evident in chapter 5 of his collected essays entitled *Structural Anthropology* (1963). Later, in an article entitled 'Le triangle culinaire' (1965), he developed the subject of cooking more clearly. In his study of myth, Levi-Strauss studied the role of fire in transforming food from the raw to the cooked state, the process he saw as marking the emergence of humanity.

To sketch the general background of anthropological contributions to the study of food and food habits, Jack Goody (1982) referred to some recent studies, particularly that of Mary Douglas, who directed attention to cooking and 'the analysis of the meal'. Although she sees food as linked to biological and social facts, it is the latter aspect that interested her when she attempted to 'decipher a meal' (1972).

A few studies of change involving historical sources and methods were made by European sociologists and anthropologists. Work on the Social history of food was not only confined to France or Western Europe but also spread to the Third World. It combines both anthropological and historical perspectives. Mintz's essay on 'Time, Sugar and. Sweetness' (1979) examined the political and economic forces behind the availability of sugar and its relationship to slavery in the Third World. Goody (1982) dealt with cooking from the point of diversified structures of households and class. The analysis of cooking, according to him, is related to the distribution of power and authority in the economic sphere, that is, to the system of class or stratification and to it's political ramification (*ibid.*, p. 37).

India has a rich history of culinary studies as evident from a number of early accounts. Mazumdar's article (1935) has at length discussed about food types and feasting as found in the different ancient texts in India. According to the *Taittiriya Upanishada*, the primary aspects of our organic existence depend upon food for its subsistence. The Rig Veda, the Buddhist literatures and Vatsyayana have described about the ideal types of food and meals.

The ancient text Ayurveda made India the only health conscious nation in the world (Kalra 1992). It prescribed a balanced and healthy diet. The text further revealed a full-fledged culinary philosophy which concerned itself with nutrition as much with taste. In fact, Indian food was considered to have both medicinal and therapeutic values.

In Assam, some early cultural information is to be had in the *Jogini Tantra*. The *Tantra* described at length about the food and food taboos of the people of Kamrupa (Neog 1966). It advised the people of Kamrupa (ancient Assam) not to give up fish and meat. A later work *Kumara-Harana* also described the different food and recipes of Assam (Achaya 1994).

Food related studies in India in the 1950s and 1960s were mostly centered on the popular theme of caste and commensality. Some of the prominent figures like Srinivas (1952), Marriott (1955b) and Dumont (1970) have to some extent followed the trend from earlier writers like Dubois (1906) and Hutton (1951).

In the 1970s, Khare made valuable theoretical contribution towards the study of food and the domestic hearth (1976a). His ethnographic study on the contemporary ways of handling food within and around the north Indian Hindu household demonstrated different aspects of the gastronomic system. It shows how food has been made meaningful culturally and socially not only for eating but also transaction. His study (1976b) raised a number of conceptual issues concerning the Hindu culinary relations and the cultural implications derived from the ideological base of the culinary system. He also observed the changes taking place to secularize food. His edited book (1992) dealing with both Hindu and Buddhist eternal food comprises many thought provoking articles on the symbolic and ritualistic aspects of food.

Studies on street food

The study of street food vending was conceived by the Equity Policy Centre, a research organization based in the USA, in 1980. The first round of study was conducted between 1982-84 in Philippines (Barth and Kuo 1984), Indonesia (Chapman 1984), Bangladesh (Owens and Hussain 1984) and Senegal (Posner 1984). The second round took place between 1984-86 in Nigeria (Kujore et al. 1986), Egypt (Loza 1985) and Thailand (Szanton and Sirisambhand 1986). These studies established the importance of informal sector to urban employment and service and highlighted the significant role that women play in the sector. After a restudy of these seven countries, a combined account of such studies along with analyses of findings, steps to improve income of vendors and safety of street food have been published by Tinker (1997).

In India, studies on street food vending have been limited. Initial references may be made to studies by Bapat (1990, 1992) and Kulkarni (1992). Bapat's studies aimed at gathering information about current policies, street food vendors, their practices and clients, food quality, nutritional value and hygiene. Kulkarni's study is an important work of licensed and unlicensed street food vendors in Pune. He studied the vendors in terms of such aspects as status, income, clientele, hygiene and food safety, etc. He tested samples of food and water from street vendors as well as restaurants and revealed that restaurant food was no more hygienic than street food. The study also emphasized the need to improve the street food sector in India.

This present work on street food vending in urban Guwahati, is a doctoral research work done at Gauhati University, Assam. It is similar to the studies conducted by Equity Policy. Centre. It explores and gathers data on a specific economic activity in the informal sector within the municipal boundary of Guwahati city. The study also considers the anthropological dimensions of caste and community factors associated with street food. So far as my knowledge goes, studies of this kind have not been done in the context of India.

This work provides a description of the nature of street food vending and other associated aspects in Guwahati city. The basic ethnographic materials, on which the study is based, were collected from a cross-section of street food vendors and customers within the municipal area of the city. Selection of the study area was made keeping in mind several factors. First, Guwahati's congenial location as the gateway to the entire north eastern India. Secondly, since historic times, Guwahati has been occupying a place of importance as a centre of political and administrative power. It has been the capital of many ruling dynasties of Assam. Thirdly, Guwahati is the premier city of the region. It is a sort of nerve centre of all urban activities and a suitable setting for the emergence and thriving of street food.

Selection of the area of study was followed by initial library work regarding existing aspects of street vending, if any, to get general understanding of the urban Unorganised Sector(UOS). The problem undertaken for study was discussed with several anthropologists, sociologists, folklorists, geographers, litterateurs and economists. Relevant information was also collected from the Health Department of the Government of Assam, Guwahati Medical College, Guwahati Municipal Corporation and Historical and Antiquarian Studies Department.

Fieldwork

Fieldwork is the backbone of anthropological studies. The first stage of fieldwork in course of this study consisted of collecting information on street foods from January to March of 1991. It was an exploratory study consisting of detailed case studies to test the feasibility of the topic. Later, in June-July 1991, the roads of the city were surveyed to identify the 'main vending areas'. The 'main vending areas' (not formally declared as vending zones by the Municipal Corporation) would imply those areas or centers where vendors gravitate naturally because there is adequate demand for the items they vend. Such vending areas or centers are near schools and colleges, hospitals, government offices, commercial areas, construction sites, motor garages, amusement centers and even residential areas. These vending areas were surveyed and in each of them, the number of vendors, nature of vending, types of food vended and the importance of each location were taken into account. This data collection drive took place for seven days at a stretch to give an almost 'static' picture of the food vending scenario in Guwahati.

After the study on the food vendors commenced, it soon became apparent that there was no ready source of information which would indicate the number of vendors operating on the streets of the city, where they were located and why they were operating as food vendors. A field survey that would generate qualitative information and also provide some quantifiable data seemed to be an appropriate step. In this stage of field work, detailed information with the help of schedules were collected from different types of street food vendors. A ‘basic information schedule’ was designed to gather both qualitative and quantitative data about the vendors and their trades. This schedule contains seven major sections. Each section is divided into several sub-sections and the questions are both open and close-ended. In addition, customers’ tastes and preferences were taken into account by interviewing a cross-section of people on whom the ‘customer survey schedule’ was administered. This stage of field work took almost one and half years to complete.

In the course of fieldwork, it was not easy to approach the vendors directly for filling in the ‘basic information schedule’. A printed schedule would upset the vendor’s natural response and put them on guard. In such a situation, conventional anthropological techniques like direct observation and informal chats proved useful. At times, the present investigator had to approach the vendors as a customer and observe ‘the activities of cooking and selling, the types of food, time of vending, location, types of customers, etc. In this manner, she had to move from vendor to vendor in an attempt to understand the vending process. These movements did not go unnoticed and evoked curiosity among the vendors. But gradually as familiarity grew and rapport was established, such curiosity disappeared. Also, explaining the purpose of visit helped dispel their doubts about her being a government or a municipal official.

Often it was seen that some of the vendors were too busy to pay attention to the investigator. Once, a vendor mistook her for a person coming to collect donation and quickly gave a five rupee note. Sometimes it so happened that several visits had to be made to meet the same vendor, but when the results were not very encouraging one felt disappointed. However, persistent efforts paid off and helped in establishing a more friendly rapport. Having said this, I would like to reiterate that there are no set formulae to conduct fieldwork. It is a process of discovery and proper training in field techniques coupled with one’s sense of ‘proper or appropriate’ behaviour will lead to a good rapport establishment.

Similarly, information about family, assets and investment were not easy to obtain. At times, to find out the role of women and children in this trade, it was necessary to question not only the vendor but also his wife. Visits to the vendor’s workplace and home to interview the wife and observe what she does brought to light many important aspects of this trade. At first, some women appeared to be uncommunicative in the presence of their men folk, but after the husbands left for work, they talked freely about their activities both at home and those related to street food.

Techniques used in field investigation

In the actual course of collecting data, several important techniques were applied. Observation proved to be one of the most important tool of data collection. All activities connected with preparing, selling and eating of different kinds of street food were observed carefully. Also, interview aided by the schedules proved to be useful. It was used to elicit information about the vendors and customers. Knowledge about the trade, communities associated with street food, recipes of food and problems faced by vendors, etc., was gathered through interview. Most of the interviews were individual interviews with the use of an interview guide. At times group interviews were taken in those places where a cluster of vendors operated. These interviews helped in cross-checking and clarifying information about migration, caste, community, traditional occupation and problems faced by vendors in Guwahati.

Case study method proved to be very effective in deriving personal information relating to the beginning of vending as a career, success and failure in street food vending, migration, etc.

Data collection through observation was supplemented with photographs. These were invaluable in reconstructing the transaction between vendors and customers. In addition, the food inventory could be meticulously and thoroughly worked out with the help of the photographs.

Universe of study

The study of any problem on scientific lines is closely related to the universe. It is a set of elements to which the procedures or measurements are to be applied. In any conventional anthropological study, the village or local community is the universe of the study. The street food vendors do not make up such a community. Ethnic homogeneity and well defined boundary of the 'community' are also lacking. Yet the vendors, constitute a definable category in view of their distinctive activity. In a way, all the street food vendors of Guwahati may be regarded as constituting the wider universe.

The exact number of street food vendors is difficult to determine. There is no municipal census of vendors. The vendors also keep changing locations frequently. Furthermore, the number of vendors increases whenever the demand for street food rises. All these factors make vendor count difficult. However, a rough estimation of the different types of food vendors may be put at around 3000. Under such circumstances, it was necessary to resort to deliberate sampling. This kind of sampling method is known as convenience sampling, where the sample is obtained by selecting convenient population units. It is suitable when the universe is not clearly defined and when complete source list is not available (Pillai and Bagavathi 1984:194).

In order to derive the sample, the main vending areas including important roads, city bus stops, transport terminals, offices, courts, hospitals, markets, educational institutions, parks, cinema halls, etc., were screened for vendor counting. While it was easy to locate the vendors who sold from fixed places, it was not possible to track all the mobile vendors for they were on the move for most times of the day. Thus, all vendors present in the main vending areas at the time of data collection have been interviewed. The sample size consists of 360 vendors including 100 stationary and 260 mobile vendors.

Every effort has been made to present in this study objective and authentic data. All data including case studies have been presented in the 'ethnographic present'. As Piddington (1957:685) noted :

> "....that we shall write in the present tense, with the reminder that this applies to the time at which the ethnographic observations were made and not to the conditions existing in the present time".

The names of persons used in the case studies are fictitious with a view to preserving the anonymity of the individuals.

Chapter Two

Food in Assamese Culture

Street food is an emerging commodity in contemporary Assam. In the earlier decades, towns in Assam, including the largest one Guwahati, were peopled mainly by the Assamese speaking Hindus and Muslims whose food habits were no different from the rural folk. Home was not merely the place for cooking food but was also the venue for eating. In the rural areas, it was only occasionally that an Assamese villager would partake tea and snacks when he visited the weekly markets or the towns in connection with work in courts and offices: However, progressive urbanization and growth of industries since about the 1950s have led to the transformation of small towns with essentially homogenous population, through migration from other parts of the country, which in turn has aided the emergence of ready-to-eat street food sector.

It would be appropriate, at this stage, to discuss in some detail the traditional Assamese food and food habits in order to understand how street food represents a new development in the context of the overall culture of food and eating habits in Assam.

GENERAL OUTLINE OF ASSAMESE FOOD

The Assamese speaking people are mainly concentrated in the Brahmaputra valley1. Their mainstay is agriculture. As rice is the staple food, paddy cultivation occupies the paramount place. There are mainly two varieties of paddy cultivated, namely, the *ahu* (summer paddy) and the *sali* (winter paddy). Among these two varieties, cultivation of *sali* paddy gets more importance. It is because the Assamese community prefers to eat rice prepared from *sali* paddy. *Ahu* is a coarse variety of paddy whereas *sali* is soft and most of the traditional light meals and snacks are prepared from the *sali* rice.

Traditionally, Assamese food is divided into three principal categories, namely - sattik (conducive to goodness), rajasik (conducive to passion) and tamasik (conducive to darkness and sloth). However, tamasik food is not common to the general people and is eaten only by the Tantric2 (Cantlie 1984:185). The Tantrics are believed to eat raw flesh and raw blood of animals sacrificed to propitiate the demons and deities. The rajasik food is common to the Assamese people which broadly mean the eating of a non-vegetarian diet. The Assamese, irrespective of caste and creed, usually take their meal along with meat, fish, egg, etc. It is the pristine rule in the Assamese society that a guest should be entertained with rice and fish, meat or egg. The sattik food restricts the eating of fish, meat and egg. It is also tabooed to eat certain pulses (masur and mati), onion, garlic, etc., for a person who is allowed to eat only the sattik food. This is because according to the Assamese tradition these foods are also included in the list of rajasik food. Generally, the high caste Hindu widows and some bhakats (devotees) take this type of food in their day-to-day life.

Meals

The Assamese meals are mainly rice based. An average Assamese person eats two meals a day, once at noon and the other at night. However, the wage earners and the agriculturists take rice three times a day: in the morning, at late noon and at night. The children take rice at any time when they feel hungry, particularly in the rural areas.

Bhat (boiled rice) is cooked in the *pakghar* or *randhani ghar* (kitchen). In every kitchen, especially in the rural areas, there are two hearths. The one on the left is used for cooking rice while the one on the right, which is comparatively smaller, is used to cook vegetables and curry. Boiled rice is cooked twice daily, once at noon and then at night. It is invariably eaten along with one or two cooked items which form the daily meals of an Assamese. One item is prepared from pulse such as mung, masur, arhar, boot or mati and the other is prepared from vegetables. Tea, snacks and light meals, termed as *jalpan*, are prepared in the *juhal* (tea room) and are taken in the early morning and again in the afternoon. It is never prepared in the kitchen so as to avoid contact with the cooking vessels used for boiling rice. It is because cooking and eating of rice are surrounded by ritual prohibition.

Though the Assamese people are basically cultivators, collecting forms another source of food supply for the rural Assamese. In addition, seasonal vegetables are grown in the kitchen garden which is a typical part of an Assamese household compound. It is said that in the olden days, before the eating of pulses became popular, Assamese people ate only vegetables and leafy vegetables with boiled rice. Today, it is usual to eat pulses along with another item prepared out of vegetables, which are either fried or made into a curry to which fish may be added.

Fish is relished by almost all the Assamese people. It is eaten in different forms by baking, boiling, drying, frying, smoking and as an ingredient in different types of *anja* (curry) like *tenga* (sour), *jola* (pungent), *khar* (alkaline), etc. It is to be noted that spicy and oily food are not generally preferred by the Assamese people. Fishing is a common activity in rural Assam. During the *sali* cultivation (water is essential for *sali* paddy), the cultivator generally catches fish from the agricultural field. In the environment of Assam, different kinds of small fishes are found wherever water accumulates for a certain period. Fish is collected for household consumption with the help of different fishing implements. Fish is also caught in the neighbouring pools, ponds, rivers, etc. During the beginning of winter season, it is a common sight in all the villages of Assam to fish individually or in groups with different fishing implements. Significantly, though the Brahmans and higher caste people of India are debarred from eating fish and meat, it is not a taboo for the higher caste people of Assam including the Brahmans. For the purpose of household consumption, fishing is not restricted to any caste and community in Assam. But fish selling is restricted according to the caste rule and allowed to only a few castes, like the Kaibartas, whose traditional occupation is fish catching and fish selling. While fish is the favourite food of the Assamese, it is never considered a snack to be eaten apart from the regular meals. Moreover, raw fish can be carried from place to place, but it can never be transported in a cooked form outside the house and is eaten only within the confines of the household3. This is because it may cause ritual pollution or *chuwa*. Thus, it is not visible even as a snack in the traditional *haat* (weekly bazaar) of Assam.

Besides fish, meat is also eaten by the Assamese people. It is not, however, eaten as frequently and widely as fish. Pigeon, duck, and goat meat are the types of meat commonly consumed. It is to be noted that in the traditional Hindu society eating of fowl is a taboo. However, nowadays, Assamese Hindus widely partake the meat of fowl in the urban areas.

The foregoing discussion provides a general picture of the Assamese meals of day-to-day life only. During festive occasions, the list of food taken with rice is more varied and elaborate. Generally, the festive food is a non-vegetarian one, except during a few rituals where such food is taboo.

Snacks and light meals

In addition to the meals, eating of light meals and snacks are also common in Assamese society. The equivalent term for a light meal in Assamese language is *jalpan*. Tea, which is a part of Assamese culture, is generally taken with homemade snacks, light meals or biscuits obtained from market. Some of the popular light meals are described below.

(a) ***Cira*** (flat rice) : It is prepared from *bara, joha, malbhog* and a few other varieties of fine paddy. The paddy is soaked for three to four hours, then strained and roasted in a dry pan. While it is still warm, the paddy is pounded to flatten it and the husk removed. Cira is a cooked *jalpan* and hence *chuwa*.

(b) ***Akhoi*** (parched rice) : Parched rice is prepared from a few varieties of fine paddy like bara, malbhog, joha, etc. The paddy is cooked in a pan filled with sand over a very hot fire till the grains burst and swell out like flowers. It is then sieved to separate the grains. This type of food is considered as uncooked and thus can be eaten by all.

(c) ***Komal chaul*** (softened rice) : It is prepared from fine varieties of paddy by boiling it over a very hot fire and then dried under the sun. After it is dried, it is pounded and the husk removed by winnowing. This parboiled rice is soaked in cold water till soft and then strained and eaten with milk or *doi* (curd) and *gur* (jaggery). Softened rice is an uncooked food (since husk remains intact during boiling) and hence not *chuwa.*

(d) ***Kecha pithaguri*** (uncooked rice flour) : It is prepared from a fine variety of rice which is soaked in cold water for a few hours. After straining, it is pounded to a fine powder. It is eaten with warm milk and jaggery along with banana. It is also used as a base for different kinds of *pitha* (rice cake). *Kecha pithaguri* is an uncooked food. However, when roasted it can be preserved for a longer period and is considered as a cooked food.

(e) **Chunga chaul** (rice cooked in the cylindrical section of green bamboo) : *Bara* rice or a fine variety of rice is stuffed in a section of green bamboo. Then sufficient water is added to it and the mouth of the cylinder is closed with banana leaf. It is then ready to be cooked over burning embers.

There are a number of snack items prepared by the Assamese. These are both sweet and savoury, some of which are described below.

(a) ***Ghila pitha*** (circular rice cake) : It is prepared from bara or any other variety of rice. The uncooked rice powder is kneaded with water, jaggery or salt and made into small balls which are flattened and fried in ghee or oil. It is categorised as cooked snack.

(b) ***Til pitha*** (rice cake with sesame) : Uncooked rice flour is spread evenly on a hot griddle. After the sides are slightly raised, a stuffing of sesame and jaggery is placed in the middle and the rice cake is rolled. This rice cake can be made with coconut stuffing also. It is a cooked snack.

(c) ***Tekeli mukhat diya pitha*** (steamed rice cake) : This cake is prepared from a fine variety of rice which is powdered and mixed with a little water and jaggery. It is then shaped into balls, flattened and is steamed over a tekeli (clay pot) of boiling water till cooked. A cake similar to this, called the bhapa pitha, is made by the immigrant Muslim community and commonly eaten by the Bihari and Muslim rickshaw and thela (pushcart) pullers in Guwahati.

(d) ***Chunga pitha*** (cake prepared in the cylindrical section of green bamboo) : This cake is prepared from the same mixture as above but cooked in a section of green bamboo over burning embers. This cake can be carried from one place to another and eaten by splitting open the bamboo.

(e) ***Boot pitha*** (a sweet of Bengal gram) : *Boot pitha* is made by parching Bengal gram and mixing it with jaggery. At first, jaggery is heated and after it melts and cools, the parched grams are added and shaped into small rounded pieces.

(f) ***Narikal laru*** (coconut balls) : The coconut is grated with the help of a *rukani* (grater) and mixed with sugar. It is then fried on a dry pan till cooked. When still warm, it is made into small balls. Coconut balls are uncooked snack because sugar is an exception to the rule of *chuwa.*

All the above mentioned light meals and snacks take a considerable time to prepare. But once prepared it can be stored over a period of time and most of them can be carried from place to place and even eaten outside of home without causing ritual pollution. All these qualities make these light meals and snacks potential street foods. Sweet cakes like *tekeli mukhat diya pitha* and *boot pitha* have already entered the market particularly in the rural weekly markets.

During the two Bihus, Assamese food could be seen at its best. Bohag Bihu which ushers in the new year (mid-April), is the beginning of the Hindu calendar year, while Magh Bihu (mid-January) indicates the completion of agricultural cycle and gathering of harvest. Bohag Bihu, the springtime Bihu, is also known as the Rongali Bihu or the festival of cheers, while Magh Bihu is called the Bhogali Bihu or the festival that one enjoys with sumptuous food. During these occasions friends and relatives are visited and entertained with a wide variety of food and snacks.

Besides the day-to-day and festive food of the Assamese, there are ritual foods that are offered to Gods, termed as *prasad* consisting of two varieties of pulses - *boot* and *mogu mah*, banana, coconut, betel nut and leaves, rice, *poka mithoi* (sweet ball prepared with uncooked rice flour and jaggery) and *payas* (rice cooked in sweetened milk).

RITUAL RULES OF COOKING AND EATING

In the Assamese Hindu social context, cooking and eating of cooked food involves rules of ritual purity and pollution. Cantlie (1984:205) has outlined two factors which govern the rules connected with the acceptance of food. First, the position of a man's caste in the hierarchy and secondly, his degree of initiation within the Vaishnava sect4. Normally, food prepared by an equal or someone superior in the caste hierarchy can make the food edible. Otherwise, it is treated as *chuwa*, made due to the touch of a low caste Hindu or a Muslim. Similarly, a whole raw fruit is not *chuwa* but once it is cut into sections it is open to ritual contamination. This makes it difficult for a higher caste Assamese or those initiated into the Vaishnava sect to partake of these foods.

Under these circumstances, cooking and eating from out-of-home sources pose difficulties. People who have to travel long distance from rural areas for work in courts and offices in the towns and cities find these restrictions difficult to follow. In the olden days, when bullock carts were used for long distance travel, people used to carry such food which can be eaten over a period of time and which is also not ritually polluting. *Komal chaul, hurum* (a kind of puffed rice), banana, curd, Bengal gram, etc., formed the main food items.

The practice of eating cooked food on the streets was never a part of Assamese culture. However, vending of cooked food by the *poharis* (women vendors) had taken place in the weekly markets. These vendors were usually the lower caste women who used to sell uncooked fish, clothing items, implements of handloom, etc., and along with these items, also used to sell *boot pitha*. Another snack, the *tekeli mukhat diya pitha* was sold in some rural markets of Assam. Today, none of these are found to be sold by Assamese vendors in the street food market of Guwahati.

From the foregoing discussion, it is clear that Assamese food encompasses a rich variety many of which have portability and durability. But despite having a wide range of food, the culture of street food could never emerge in the traditional rural society. One can speculate upon this. Food in the Assamese ethos was something generally eaten in the context of one's home or in the house of a person with equal or higher caste status. The concept of eating out, in the road or from roadside eateries, could not develop because mobility of Assamese people was mostly limited to short distance visits to relatives, friends or nearby market places. So, the scope of eating food outside home rarely arose. Also, in case of long distance travel, only such food were carried which were ritually pure and could not acquire impurity even during travel. Overall, conceptions of purity and pollution and caste norms regulated the kind of foods that could be eaten, under different circumstances and what kind of foods could be transported.

Notes

1. 'The Brahmaputra valley is an alluvial plain, 725 kms. long and about 80 kms. broad on the average and consists of an area of 56,339 sq. kms.
2. Tantricism is a form of Hinduism which evolved around the Kamakhya temple in Guwahati. It is associated with magic and witchcraft, animal sacrifices and occult practices.
3. In Assamese Hindu culture, cooking implies subjecting a food to heating process which makes it restrictive. Soaking of food in water also makes certain food pervious to *chuwa* (ritual contamination). The degree of *chuwa* depends upon several factors - for instance the presence or absence of the outer cover of grains, fruits or vegetables. If boiled or soaked with the protective covering, the *chuwa* is less. Secondly, addition of oil and salt to the boiled food makes it more *chuwa*. However, sweet things (sugar, honey and jaggery) and food prepared from milk and milk products are free from ritual pollution. For details about ritual contamination in Assamese food, see Cantlie 1984.
4. The Vaishnava movement in Assam, spread by the saint-poet Sankardeva (1449-1569 AD), shaped the religious, cultural and social life of the Assamese. Vaishnavism which he preached was a progressive and reformist movement against the excess of Hindu ritualism. Vaishnavism owes allegiance to Lord Krishna who is considered the Supreme being.

Chapter - 3

Guwahati city- The Setting

As already indicated, street food is intimately linked with progressive urban and industrial growth. It calls for an expanding market economy, a growing heterogenous population and presence of people who otherwise lack provisions of cooking and eating where they reside.

The state of Assam (area: 78,438 sq. Km.) in the north eastern part of India (Fig. 1) has a population of 22,414,322 persons according to the 1991 census. The state has always been characterized by a high degree of immigration from other parts of the country going back to practically the inception of British colonial rule in 1826. During the colonial period, encouraged by the British administrators and the need of the economy, a large number of people having distinct language, culture and ethnic backgrounds came to the region (Bhagabati 1992:18).

From 1830s till about the 1950s, a large number of migrants flooded the state particularly from the neighbouring states of Bengal, Bihar and Orissa. In 1831, when Bengali became the language of Assam, a large number of Bengali-speaking Hindu people from the neighbouring province of Bengal came and occupied petty jobs in administration and as teachers in vernacular and Anglo-vernacular schools of Assam. In 1881, with the coming of the railways into Assam and its subsequent expansion, Bengali people were largely absorbed into this sector. Another stream of migrants, the rural peasants from erstwhile East Pakistan (now Bangladesh), who were predominantly Muslims came in large numbers and occupied the uninhabited char (riverine tracts) of the fertile Brahmaputra valley (*ibid.*).

In the middle of the nineteenth century, tribal people from southern Bihar, Bengal, eastern Uttar Pradesh, Orissa and even from far away Andhra Pradesh and Tamil Nadu came to work as labourers in the tea gardens now numbering about 800 and contributing 15 per cent of the world's production of tea. These migrant labourers along with their locally born descendants constitute an important section of the present population of Assam.

During the same period, the Nepali people came from Nepal as part of the colonial army and as graziers. Today, they control the milk, trade in the state. This period also saw immigration of the Marwari people (from Rajasthan) who came and settled in different parts of the state, playing a key role in trading and commercial activities. In fact, they act as money changers and control the wholesale trade in food, textile, hardware, etc.

All these migrant groups of people (otherwise unknown in this area) having diverse linguistic, cultural and social background have contributed to the ethnic diversity of the state. Apart from a small section of people working as clerks, officers, teachers, etc., the majority were rural cultivators and plantation workers. Though they brought with them the diversity of culture and of food habits, these migrants were not capable of supporting or patronizing street food. This is largely because home was their place of work as well as stay.

The end of colonial rule in 1947 and the progressive industrialization since about the 1950s, led to an increase in the growth of urban population in Assam from 3,45,000 in 1951 to 24,88,000 in 1991, including 93 towns and the city of Guwahati. The rural-urban distribution of the people, according to 1991 census reveals that only 11.1 per cent of the people reside in urban areas as compared to 26 per cent in India as a whole. This makes Assam one of the least urbanized states in India with Guwahati as the only city in the entire region.

Guwahati, the capital of Assam and the headquarter of Kamrup district, is located on a crescent shaped foot hill plain skirting the river Brahmaputra (Fig. 1). The city extends from east to west for about 35 kms., from Chandrapur to Dharapur. Its north - south extension from the riverbank to Khanapara is about 15 kms. in the middle and about 6 kms. in its western margin. The city is restricted in the south by the Meghalaya foothills. In fact, a large number of hills and hillocks are scattered within the Guwahati Municipal Corporation itself. Of these, Ramcha hills, Chaatrachal and Karnachal commonly known as Chandmari hills complex, Sarania hills, Narakasur, Kalapahar, Nilachal, Fatasil hillock and Tetelia Boragaon hillocks are the major ones. These hills, hillocks and the swamps lying at their feet often restrict the growth of settlement and roads within the city. There are a few hill streams of which Bharalu is the main. It has a small tributary called Bonda that joins it from the east near the Assam State Zoo.

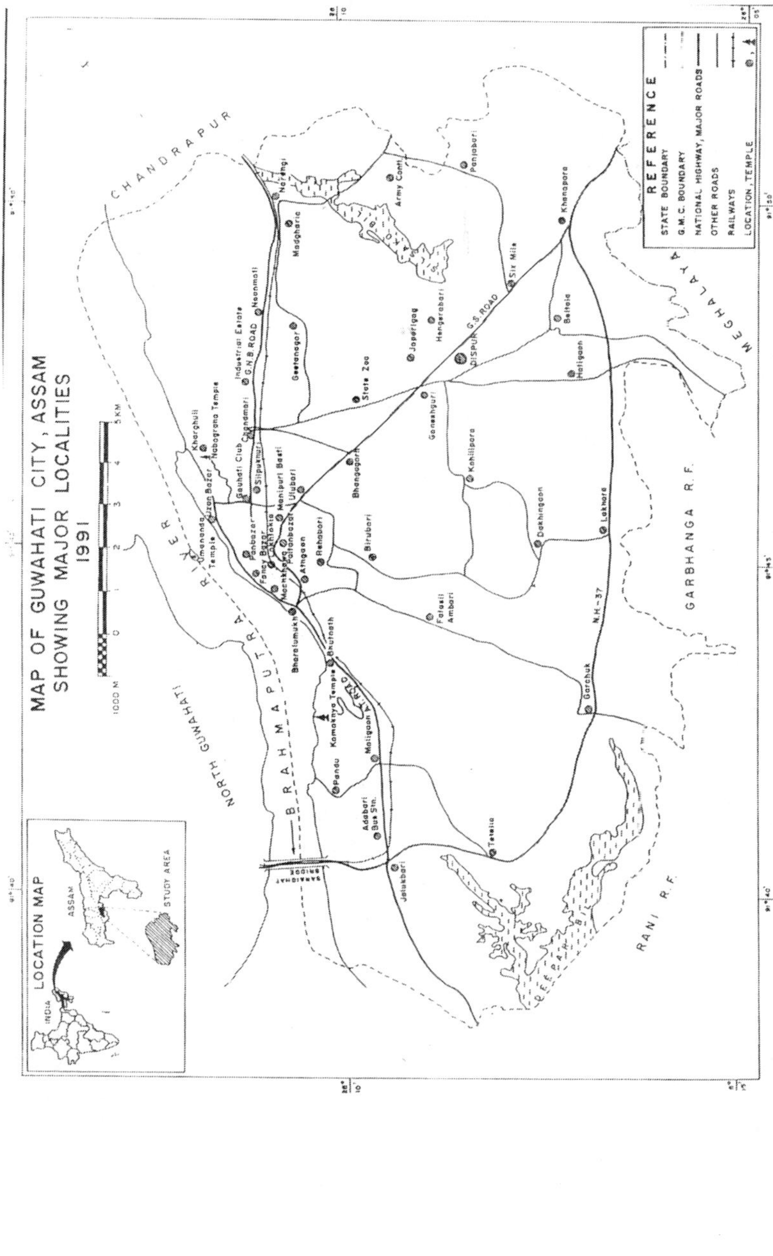
MAP OF GUWAHATI CITY, ASSAM
SHOWING MAJOR LOCALITIES
1991
LOCATION MAP
INDIA
ASSAM
STUDY AREA
REFERENCE
STATE BOUNDARY
G.M.C. BOUNDARY
NATIONAL HIGHWAY, MAJOR ROADS
OTHER ROADS
RAILWAYS
LOCATION, TEMPLE
BRAHMAPUTRA RIVER
NORTH GUWAHATI
CHANDRAPUR
MEGHALAYA
GARBHANGA R.F.
RANI R.F.
G.N.B. ROAD
G.S. ROAD
N.H.-37
Saraighat Bridge
Jalukbari
Adabari Bus Stn.
Pandu
Maligaon
Kamakhya Temple
Bharalumukh
Bhutnath
Machkhowa
Fancy Bazar
Panbazar
Paltanbazar
Athgaon
Rehabari
Uzan Bazar
Umananda Temple
Gauhati Club
Chandmari
Silpukhuri
Kharghuli
Nabagraha Temple
Manipuri Basti
Ulubari
Bhangagarh
Birubari
Fatasil Ambari
Industrial Estate
Geetanagar
Noonmati
Madgharia
Narangi
Army Cantt.
State Zoo
Japorigog
Hengerabari
DISPUR
Ganeshguri
Kahilipara
Dakhingaon
Lakhara
Garchuk
Tetelia
Beltola
Hatigaon
Six Mile
Khanapara
Panjabari

History of the Development of the City

The modern city of Guwahati (ancient Pragjyotishpur) has a rich historical background which is reflected in the past and present urbanization of the city. Ancient Guwahati was the flourishing capital of many dynasties from known period of history till the downfall of the Pala dynasty in the 12th century A.D. During the Ahom period (1228 AD. - 1839 AD.) Guwahati became the sub-capital (the capital was Gargaon in the present Sibsagar district), and remained so throughout the long period of its administration.

After the British occupation of Assam in 1826 the pace of development of Guwahati became rapid. It became the headquarter of the British Commissioner of the Brahmaputra valley till 1847 when Assam was constituted into a province under a Chief Commissioner and its capital was established at Shillong in the Khasi hills, about 100 kms. south of Guwahati. The district headquarter, administrative offices and military cantonment were established here. This led to the increase of town dwellers requiring public utility services to cater to the needs of the people of Guwahati. In 1865, Guwahati became a municipal town with the establishment of a Municipal Board in the same year. After independence, Guwahati began to grow due to the establishment of major institutions of higher education and of administrative offices and expansion of trade and commerce. Today, the city has become the most important administrative, commercial, economic, cultural, political and educational centre of north-eastern India (Fig. 2).

Commercially, Guwahati began to attain importance after the independence of the country in 1947. Its economic significance increased further after becoming the capital of Assam in 1972. Since then, economic and industrial activities in the city accelerated. Although the importance of Guwahati is mainly administrative, its physical location within the north-eastern region as also of the country as a whole has led to a growth in commerce and industries, thus attracting a large number of people.

Being the principal city of the region, it has rail, road and air links with the rest of the country. Before the introduction of railways and motor transport in the region Guwahati, being situated on the bank of the Brahmaputra, was an important river port. The water route through this river was used to transport both passengers and goods from Calcutta in West Bengal up to Dibrugarh in Assam via Guwahati. After construction of the Saraighat bridge - the first river bridge over Brahmaputra in 1962, linking the city to its north bank - the importance of this riverine route declined.

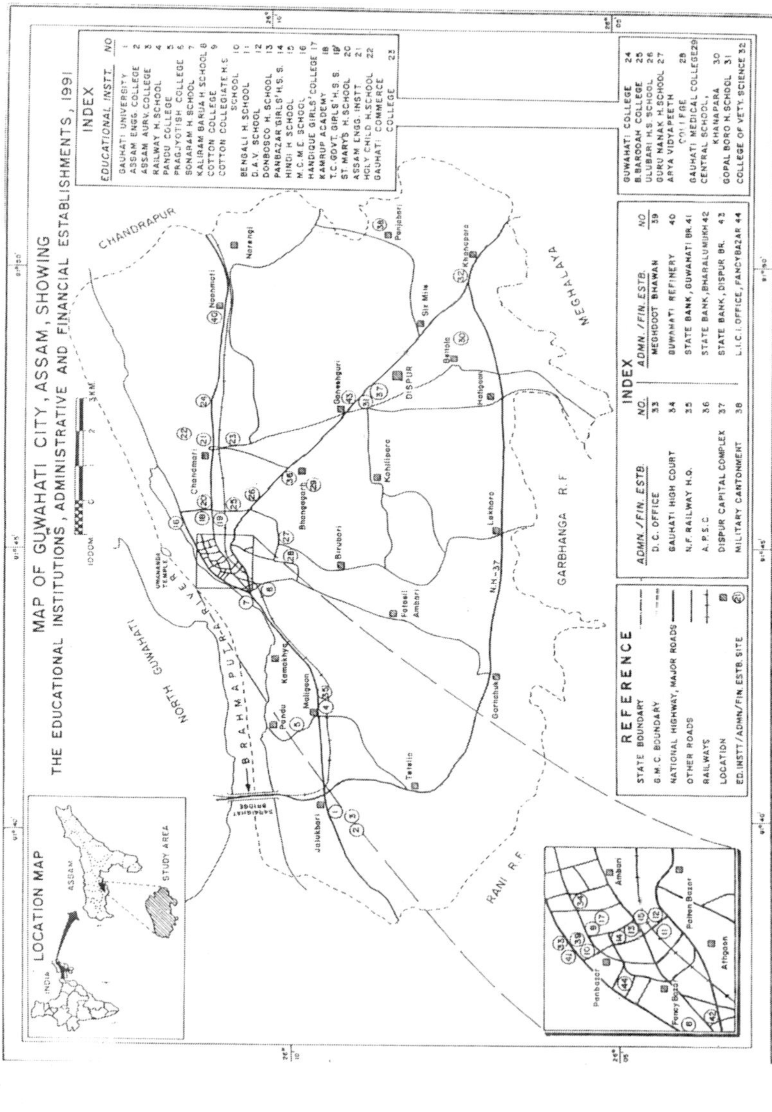

MAP OF GUWAHATI CITY, ASSAM, SHOWING
THE EDUCATIONAL INSTITUTIONS, ADMINISTRATIVE AND FINANCIAL ESTABLISHMENTS, 1991
LOCATION MAP
INDIA
ASSAM
STUDY AREA
INDEX
EDUCATIONAL INSTT. NO
GAUHATI UNIVERSITY 1
ASSAM ENGG. COLLEGE 2
ASSAM AURV. COLLEGE 3
RAILWAY H. SCHOOL 4
PANDU COLLEGE 5
PRAGJYOTISH COLLEGE 6
SONARAM H. SCHOOL 7
KALIRAM BARUA H. SCHOOL 8
COTTON COLLEGE 9
COTTON COLLEGIATE H.S. SCHOOL 10
BENGALI H. SCHOOL 11
D.A.V. SCHOOL 12
DONBOSCO H. SCHOOL 13
PANBAZAR GIRLS' H.S. S. 14
HINDI H. SCHOOL 15
M.C.M.E. SCHOOL 16
HANDIQUE GIRLS' COLLEGE 17
KAMRUP ACADEMY 18
T.C. GOVT. GIRLS' H.S. S. 19
ST. MARY'S H. SCHOOL 20
ASSAM ENGG. INSTT. 21
HOLY CHILD H. SCHOOL 22
GAUHATI COMMERCE COLLEGE 23
GUWAHATI COLLEGE 24
B. BAROOAH COLLEGE 25
ULUBARI H.S. SCHOOL 26
GURU NANAK H. SCHOOL 27
ARYA VIDYAPEETH COLLEGE 28
GAUHATI MEDICAL COLLEGE 29
CENTRAL SCHOOL, KHANAPARA 30
GOPAL BORO H. SCHOOL 31
COLLEGE OF VETY. SCIENCE 32
INDEX
ADMN./FIN. ESTB. NO.
D. C. OFFICE 33
GAUHATI HIGH COURT 34
N.F. RAILWAY H.Q. 35
A.P.S.C. 36
DISPUR CAPITAL COMPLEX 37
MILITARY CANTONMENT 38
ADMN./FIN. ESTB. NO
MEGHDOOT BHAWAN 39
GUWAHATI REFINERY 40
STATE BANK, GUWAHATI BR. 41
STATE BANK, BHARALUMUKH 42
STATE BANK, DISPUR BR. 43
L.I.C.I. OFFICE, FANCYBAZAR 44
REFERENCE
STATE BOUNDARY
G.M.C. BOUNDARY
NATIONAL HIGHWAY, MAJOR ROADS
OTHER ROADS
RAILWAYS
LOCATION
ED. INSTT/ADMN/FIN. ESTB. SITE
NORTH GUWAHATI
BRAHMAPUTRA RIVER
CHANDRAPUR
MEGHALAYA
GARBHANGA R.F.
RANI R.F.
N.H.-37
UMANANDA TEMPLE
SARAIGHAT BRIDGE
Jalukbari
Pandu
Maligaon
Kamakhya
Fatasil Ambari
Birubari
Bhangagarh
Chandmari
Noonmati
Narangi
Panjabari
Ganeshguri
DISPUR
Kahilipara
Beltola
Hatigaon
Sixmile
Khanapara
Lakhara
Garchuk
Tetelia
Panbazar
Fancy Bazar
Paltan Bazar
Athgaon
Ambari

Fig 2

The coming of the railways to Guwahati1 and construction of the national highway No. 37 in the 1960s, linking Guwahati to different states of the region and the country, led to a tremendous increase of commercial activity in the city. Guwahati is the main receiving and distributing centre of goods for the entire north eastern region. Most of the goods are either carried by truck or rail-transport. At present about 4000 trucks and buses enter the city daily. The railways also play a major role in the transportation of passengers and goods. With the extension of broad gauge line to Guwahati in April, 1984 both passenger and goods traffic have increased[2].

Industrially, Assam is a backward state, yet the industrial importance of Guwahati is significant. It has a number of medium and small industries and also a large industry in the public sector, namely Guwahati Refinery at Noonmati situated to the east of the city (Fig. 2). There are various types of small industries associated with fabrication, brick making, saw milling and carpentry, welding and riveting, bakery and food processing, plastic goods manufacturing and other works associated with cottage industries which attract a large number of labourers (skilled and unskilled) and buyers, etc. It is such development which is responsible for creating the demand for street food in Guwahati.

Guwahati also enjoys the distinction of being an important religious, educational and cultural centre of Assam. The famous Shakta temple of Mother Goddess Kamakhya built in 1565 A.D.[3] is located atop the Nilachal hills in Guwahati. There are numerous other shrines like Nabagraha, Sukreswar, Ugratara, Umananda, Basistha, etc., which attract a large number of pilgrims and devotees. During the great fair of ambubashi (a period when the earth is believed to be menstruating) held in the precincts of the Kamakhya temple in June-July, people throng to visit the temple from all parts of India. In addition, Shivratri fair in Umananda temple held during February-March also attracts a large number of people. The congregation of people during such fairs and festivals provides suitable locales for street food vendors. Besides the above mentioned temples, there are a large number of mosques, churches and gurudwaras scattered all over the city, where street food vendors setup stalls during the religious festivals.

From the point of view of education, Guwahati has been a centre of formal learning in the region for a very long time. The first ever high school in Assam, namely Cotton Collegiate High School (presently a higher secondary school) was established by the government in the year 1834 and the first college, Cotton College was established in 1901. For a very long time this remained the only college of Assam. At present, as a single urban area, Guwahati has the- highest number of educational institutions in the whole of north-east India (Bhagabati et. al. 1986:14). Today, there are about 100 educational institutions in Guwahati (Fig. 2).

Parks and open spaces are limited in Guwahati. There is one park called Nehru Park near the Deputy Commissioner's Court, which attracts a large number of children and adults. Other parks worth mentioning are the Mahabir Jain park, Shankardev park, Tarun Ram Phukan park, etc. Apart from these, a few play grounds like the Judges' field near Nehru park, New Field in Paltan Bazar, Dispur Parade Ground, Assam Engineering Institute field in Chandmari and Latasil field near the High Court are available for sporting activities. Besides using these fields for sports, they are often used for holding exhibitions, fairs, circus, public meetings, etc. There are two major stadia in Guwahati - The Nehru stadium (capacity: 30,000) to the east of the city is used for holding major events like football and cricket. In addition, the N.F. Railway has a smaller stadium (capacity: 10,000) to the west of the city at Maligaon. The Assam State Zoo, located in the eastern side of the city attracts many people throughout the year not only from Guwahati, but from all over the state. There are 16 cinema halls in Guwahati which provide recreation to its people. All the above mentioned centres of recreation like parks and play grounds, zoo, cinema halls, etc., are the points where street food sellers gravitate (Fig. 3). It is here that a variety of food vendors sell their relishes and snacks catering to the tastes and preferences of the people.

There are as many as 24 important daily markets situated in different localities of the city (Fig. 4). There are two weekly markets at Beltola and at Maligaon provide vegetables, fish, meat, clothing, utensils and other miscellaneous items. These weekly markets, particularly the Beltola bazar, are visited by people even from faraway places. It is in such locations that the street food vendors-provide an important service by selling ready-to-eat food for the benefit of both buyers and sellers.

Population growth

Census figures of population as recorded in 1872 gives a total population of 11,492 for the town. It increased marginally to 11,695 persons in 1881. In 1891, the population declined to 8,283. The reason is attributed to a kalazar epidemic which broke out in Guwahati in 1888. From 1901 onwards the population steadily increased as shown in Table 1.

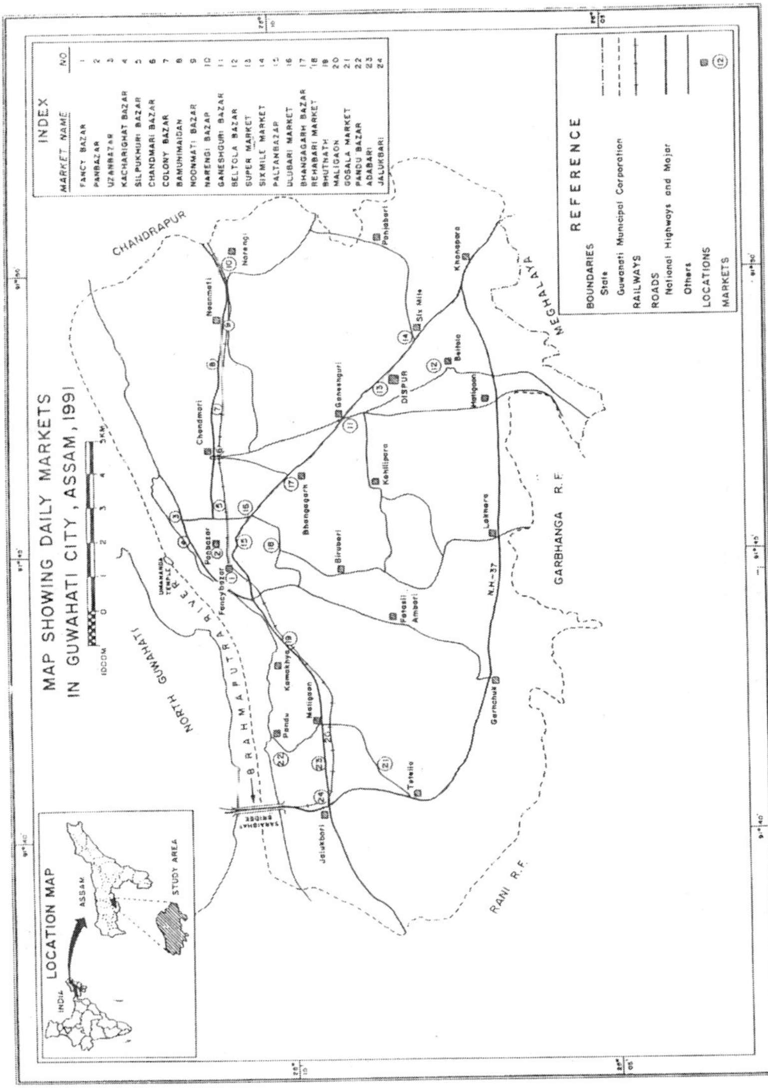

MAP SHOWING DAILY MARKETS
IN GUWAHATI CITY, ASSAM, 1991
INDEX
MARKET NAME NO
FANCY BAZAR 1
PANBAZAR 2
UZANBAZAR 3
KACHARIGHAT BAZAR 4
SILPUKHURI BAZAR 5
CHANDMARI BAZAR 6
COLONY BAZAR 7
BAMUNIMAIDAN 8
NOONMATI BAZAR 9
NARENGI BAZAR 10
GANESHGURI BAZAR 11
BELTOLA BAZAR 12
SUPER MARKET 13
SIXMILE MARKET 14
PALTANBAZAR 15
ULUBARI MARKET 16
BHANGAGARH BAZAR 17
REHABARI MARKET 18
BHUTNATH 19
MALIGAON 20
GOSALA MARKET 21
PANDU BAZAR 22
ADABARI 23
JALUKBARI 24
REFERENCE
BOUNDARIES
State
Guwahati Municipal Corporation
RAILWAYS
ROADS
National Highways and Major
Others
LOCATIONS
MARKETS
LOCATION MAP
INDIA
ASSAM
STUDY AREA
CHANDRAPUR
NORTH GUWAHATI
BRAHMAPUTRA RIVER
UMANANDA TEMPLE
SARAIGHAT BRIDGE
MEGHALAYA
GARBHANGA R.F.
RANI R.F.
N.H.-37
DISPUR
Narengi
Noonmati
Chandmari
Ganeshguri
Six Mile
Khanapara
Panjabari
Beltola
Hatigaon
Kahilipara
Bhangagarh
Lokhara
Birubari
Fatasil Ambari
Panbazar
Fancybazar
Kamakhya
Maligaon
Pandu
Tetelia
Garchuk
Jalukbari

Fig 4

Table 3.1: Urban Population Growth in Guwahati (1901-1991).

Year	*Population*	*Decadal variation*
1901	11,661	
1911	12,481	+ 7.03
1921	16,480	+ 32.04
1931	21,797	+ 32.26
1941	29,598	+ 35.49
1951	84,601	+ 185.83
1961	1,66,695	+ 97.04
1971	2,52,305	+ 51.36
1981*	-	-
1991	5,84,342	+ 131.60

** 1981 census could not be conducted in Assam, owing to the situation prevailing at that time.*
*(**Source** : Census of India 1981, Series 3 part X-A and Statistical Hand bock, Assam 1993, Guwahati, Directorate of Economics and Statistics).*

Table 3.1 show that in the first decade the population of Guwahati increased marginally (7.03%). In 1921, the population increased suddenly and continued till 1951 to an all time high of 185.83 per cent. This increase can be attributed to the expansion of the municipal boundary to 7.7 sq. kms., incursion of population from Bengal to Assam and general flow of migrants following the independence of the country in 1947. The decennial growth of population from 1951-1971 may be attributed to several factors such as immigration, establishment of the North East Frontier Railway headquarter at Maligaon, Oil refinery at Noonmati, several educational institutions and expansion of town area to 14.08 sq. kms. Between 1971-1991, there was a tremendous growth of population primarily because of the transfer of capital from Shillong to Guwahati, associated administrative expansion and growing commercial and industrial importance. In 1974, with the establishment of Gauhati Municipal Corporation, Guwahati became the first and only city of the region. The increase of population in 1991 census after twenty years cannot be said to be as high as that of 1951 and 1961 census. However, with the present growth rate of 131.60 per cent with a high density of population of 2,695 persons per sq. km., Guwahati has become one of the most crowded cities of Eastern India (Bhattacharyya 1990:5-9).

Adding to the already existing population, Guwahati attracts a large number of people daily for administrative, business and educational purposes. Every day, thousands of people pour into the city from the neighbouring villages, towns and districts by bus, ferry and train to school, college, and office and business establishments in the city. In the evening, there is an exodus of these people. It is this transient section of people who leave their homes early in the morning and return late in the evening who have to depend upon quick and cheap ready-to-eat street food during the day. Moreover, long distance travellers who arrive in the city in the early morning or late at night are to a large extent dependent on the street corner tea stalls or roadside pushcarts for their cup of tea or a quick meal.

Settlement pattern and ethnic composition

Territorially, Guwahati has expanded to keep pace with the increase, in population. The early settlements concentrated mainly in the region between the Brahmaputra in the north and the railway line in the south4. Later, in the 1950's and 1960's, settlements spread further south to Kalapahar. New settlements cropped up in Sarania, Gandhibasti, Lachit Nagar, Santipur, etc.

Around the same time a railway township came up at Maligaon followed by the Gauhati University campus to the west of the former. All these developed over the plains skirting the Brahmaputra. In the 1970s, when the pressure of population further increased, the city expanded to include Beltola plains through a corridor in the south of the city. Side by side settlements also came up at Fatasil, Noonmati, Khanapara, Dispur, Basistha, Kahilipara, etc.

In Guwahati, most of the localities except the new residential areas have a homogenous residential pattern. The tendency is to make settlement along caste or community lines. This is true in the old areas of the city such as Uzanbazar, Chenikuthi, Bharalumukh, Shantipur and Rehabari which are primarily inhabited by the caste Hindus. Assamese Muslims are mainly concentrated in Hedayatpur, Machkhowa and Lakhtokia. The Bengali Muslims are distributed in Dhirenpara, Fatasil-Ambari, etc. The Christians are located in Christian Basti and the Sikhs are scattered over Fancy bazar, Paltanbazar, Hatigaon, Milanpur and Beltola areas. The main commercial centre of Fancy bazar, Panbazar and Paltan bazar are inhabited by Marwaris from Rajasthan (who are primarily Jains), Assamese and Bengali people respectively. There is a small pocket of Manipuri people found in the Manipuri basti near Paltan bazar. The Nepali people are found in the fringe areas of the city near Khanapara in Amerigog in the Assam-Meghalaya border.

In case of the newly developed residential areas the populations are of mixed ethnic background. It is important to mention that there are no completely residential areas in the city except a few areas like the Oil India Limited and Assam State Electricity Board Complexes at Narengi, Railway colony at Maligaon and Bamunimaidam, Gauhati University Campus at Jalukbari, a campus of Assam Agricultural University at Khanapara, Temporary Capital Complex at Dispur and a few multi-storied flats scattered over the city. The rest are either mixed residential, i.e., residential localities having commercial establishments and commercial areas which are predominantly market and office areas.

Besides the above mentioned settlements, the city is composed of several areas of sub-standard living conditions. These include slums and blighted areas. In the northern part of the city, at Kharghuli near Uzanbazar, there is an area of substandard living condition. It is inhabited by rickshaw pullers, street food vendors primarily of Bihari origin, part time housemaids and other informal sector workers. They also live in scattered locations in Maligaon, Pandu and Noonmati areas. More areas of sub-standard living can also be found in Kachari basti in Ulubari, a few pockets in Paltanbazar,

B. Barooah Road and in Fatasil Ambari. These areas are inhabited predominantly by sweepers whose colonies were made by the Guwahati Municipal Corporation. Some areas in the southern part of the city of Athgaon, Fatasil-Ambari, Birubari and in the central part of Paltanbazar are mostly inhabited by street food vendors, thela, rickshaw pullers and daily wage earners. Over and above the areas mentioned, there is a slum area on either side of the railway line from Ambari to Fancy bazar (except the Guwahati Railway Station) and below the Panbazar over bridge. The living conditions in these areas are deplorable. These are mostly inhabited by informal sector workers including street food vendors.

Most of the houses inhabited by the street food vendors in the above mentioned sub-standard areas are rented accommodation. They are of thatched roofs with bamboo or reed walls and earthen floor. There is no drainage, garbage disposal, sewerage or drinking water facility in these areas. The living condition of these people is very poor. They utilize the same room for dwelling and cooking purposes. During rainy season, these houses and roads are partially submerged with dirty water making the conditions very unhygienic.

Urban infrastructure and facility

In order to understand the life of the people living in Guwahati, mention must be made of the various civic facilities and other amenities available to its people.

(i) **Road network and transport system**: Being the only city in the region, the existing road network shows lack of any form or pattern. The majority (53%) of the roads are non-metalled as compared to black-topped roads (35%). Also, there is no uniformity in the width of the roads. Except for the G.S. Road and parts of A.T. Road, majority of the roads are narrow leading to overcrowding and congestion particularly in the busy commercial areas.

Guwahati has a good network of city bus service operating along the important roads of the city. They are run by both private operators and the government. They serve as a very important means of commuter traffic in the city. Besides the city bus, auto-rickshaws and slow moving rickshaws form a part the of urban transport system in Guwahati.

Another mode of mass transport, the ferry service, facilitates movement of people between north bank and the main city in the south bank. Though city bus service exists via the Saraighat bridge, it is not frequent and thus inconvenient to daily commuters who are mainly dependent upon the ferry service[5].

(ii) **Drainage system**: The city at present does not have any scientific drainage system. Some of the areas are served by a system of pucca (cemented) road-side drains. Yet the system is not effective. Most of the main roads of the city are provided with foot path cum major drains which are lacking in planning and an integrated approach. In most of the localities including the new residential areas, the drainage system is poor. There are no drains in the sub-standard living areas, and if at all, these are *kutcha* (earthen).

The natural topography of Guwahati is such that rain water is carried by river Bharalu through Khanajan river in the west and discharged into the Brahmaputra river. However, because of over-population and rapid increase of built up area' (by filling up uninhabitable low lying areas and cutting down hills, etc.) the existing capacities of these natural channels have been reduced, leading to frequent flooding and water logging of most of the low lying areas of the city.

(iii) **Water supply and drinking water facility**: The main source of water supply for Guwahati is the Brahmaputra River. The city needs 156 million litres of water per day. But the different sources like the Guwahati Municipal Corporation, the Public Health Engineering Department, Urban Water and Sewerage Board, the

Guwahati Refinery and the N.F. Railway together can supply only about 90 million litres of water per day.

The city does not have any integrated water supply system to cover the entire area. The government has been able to provide drinking water through the Guwahati Municipal Coporation to only 48.5 per cent of the total population. The rest uses ring well (36.1%), tube well or deep tube well (13.5%) and natural sources (0.2%) like ponds, etc. (Bora 1997).

(iv) **Sewage and garbage disposal:** Guwahati city have no underground sewerage system except for railway, refinery and defence areas. Majority of the households under Guwahati Municipal Corporation have individual septic tank system without any collective disposal of affluent. In many of the sub-standard and slum areas already mentioned there is no proper system of disposal of night soil. The conservancy system of service latrines is still followed in these areas.

Regarding general garbage there is again no scientific approach. All garbage and waste materials are kept on the road sides which are carried away and dumped in open space near Fatasil-Ambari, emitting foul smell and largely affecting the environment[6].

In this chapter, we have attempted to give an outline of Guwahati as an ideal setting for the emergence and growth of street food vending. From the discussion made in this chapter, it is clear that Guwahati's importance as an administrative, educational, economic and political centre has aided the growth of street food sector.

In Chapter Four, some popular varieties of street food vended in Guwahati have been discussed.

Notes

1. The railway line to Guwahati came to North Guwahati in 1952. However, after the construction of Saraighat bridge, the railway line came up to Guwahati city in 1964.
2. According to an estimate, the volume of passengers coming to Guwahati has been put at 21.2 million in 1991-92. This increased to 26.5 million in 1994-95. Also, the volume of goods unloaded in Guwahati in 1994-95 (both broad and meter gauge) is 1,200,492 tonnes. This increased to 1,855,529 tonnes in 1995-96 (Source: N.F. Railway).
3. It is not known with certainty when this temple was originally built. Archaeologist put the date to the 8th Century. The original temple was destroyed by Kalapahar, a Bengali Hindu convert to Islam and rebuilt by the Koch king Naranarayan in the year 1566 A.D.

4. Guwahati can mainly be divided into two parts - northern and southern, by the railway line which passes through the city in an east-west direction. The northern part is comparatively higher than the southern part.
5. It is estimated that in 1991-92, through the three main points in North Guwahati, viz., North Guwahati, Madhyam Khanda and Rajaduar, riverine ferry has carried 891 thousand passengers to the city (Source : Statistical Handbook, Assam. 1993. Directorate of Economics and Statistics, Guwahati).
6. The built-up area in the city has been expanding in a devastating manner despite the fact that only 22.1 per cent of the Guwahati Municipal Corporation area is fit for construction activity. In 1968, the built-up area in the city was 26.8 per cent and in 1990 it reached 42.2 per cent (Patowary 1997).

Chapter - 4

Street Food Varieties in Guwahati

India is a land of varied cultures and inevitably food also varies from region to region. It is influenced not only by the physical environment but by custom and religion as well. Food, particularly cooked food, has always been deeply entrenched in the culture, religion and ethos of different communities and societies of India. Cooking and partaking of cooked food are not merely connected with satisfaction of hunger but also fulfilment of cultural conditions and prescriptions. In the Hindu society considerations of caste and commensal ban across caste lines have been of great importance in the consumption of cooked food1. Given the predominantly rural character of the Indian population (74% in the 1991 census) and the essentially agricultural nature of its economy, the culture of eating out and patronizing commercial eateries have been limited to towns and cities.

Assam too, is largely rural, where 89 per cent of its total population still lives in rural areas. Here, cultural, religious and other social factors play determining roles with regard to cooking and eating of food. The more conservative among the Assamese Hindus still adhere to the traditional taboos and restrictions while eating cooked food.

There are, however, some foods which transcend all restrictions associated with the process of eating. These are sweetmeats and food prepared from milk and its products. As with the rest of the country, even in Assam, eating of sweetmeat in places outside home is permissible. Such food can be carried from place to place and when people visit relatives, it is customary to carry food hampers of home cooked sweetmeats and other edibles. However, none of these ready-to-eat Assamese sweetmeats and snacks which can be transported and preserved has graduated to street food.

The selling of ready-to-eat food in the street is a highly visible activity in many cities of the world. In a developing country like India, selling of street food in towns and cities is a ubiquitous activity. This feature is true not only for a developing country like India, but is a growing phenomenon even in the "developed" cities (Tinker 1994). In India, street food vendors in a city like Pune (population 16 lakhs in 1991) in Maharashtra sells as many as 95 varieties of food (Kulkarni 1992). In Guwahati too (population 5.84 lakhs in 1991), vendors sell a variety of street food. A count taken in 1991 showed that as many as 55 varieties of street food were sold in Guwahati. These include an array of different sweet, salted and spicy items some of which are snacks while others range from light to full scale meals. In addition, tea, different types of fruits, fruit juices and ice sticks also constitute a part of ready-to-eat food2. Fig. 5 gives the frequency of street food vendors according to varieties of food sold.

TYPES OF STREET FOOD

There is a wide variety of street food prepared and sold in Guwahati. These may broadly be divided into five different types: relishes, snacks and light meals, sweetmeats, fruits and juices and meals. Each of these is addressed to a specific type of clientele and has its own unique niche in the street food arena. A description of the different types of food is given below.

Relishes

These are the spicy, salty, sweet and sour food which are eaten largely to satisfy the palate and can be had at any time of the day. Usually, these are served with a distinctive taste and flavour. These edibles are inherently street food in the sense that these are more appealing only when eaten in the street. These include hot roasted *chana* (chick peas), *jhalmuri* (spicy puffed rice), *phuska* (little dough puffs filled with a sour, peppery liquid) and *bhelpuri* (mixture of crushed dough crisps, puffed rice, sweet and sour chutney, chilli and fragrant coriander leaves), etc. The relishes are often always sold by the itinerant vendors who belong to the Bihari community. They move about from place to place during the day in a definite route and finally in the evening stall themselves in a convenient spot. In fact, their visibility and accessibility create their own demand. Some of the popular relishes sold in Guwahati are described below.

Chanachur (a crisp, fried and parched relish): It is a crisp mixture of fried and parched grams, to which are added peanuts, flat rice, fried gram flour noodles, roasted maize grains, etc. These ingredients are mixed together in a spicy, tangy mixture by adding chopped onions, green chillies, fresh coriander leaves and a dash of lime. This mixture is made piquant

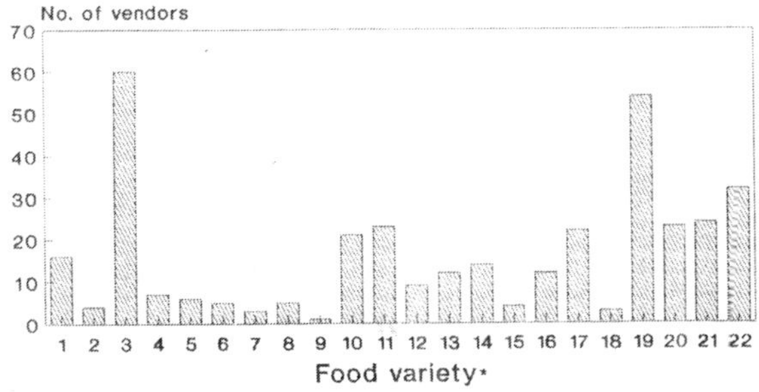

FIG. 5. FREQUENCY OF STREET FOOD VENDORS ACCORDING TO VARIETIES OF FOOD SOLD

*Legends:

No.	Item
1	*Bhelpuri*
2	Boiled eggs
3	*Chanachur*
4	Chips
5	*Chat*
6	Chowmein, *pulao*, roll, *ghugni*, etc.
7	Corn
8	Curd
9	*Dosa*
10	Fruit slices
11	Groundnut
12	*Hawa mithai*, *pankha mithai*
13	*Jhalmuri*
14	Juice
15	*Kulfi*
16	*Laddu*
17	*Phuska*
18	*Pakora*
19	Sweetmeat
20	Tea, bun, biscuit, cake, etc.
21	Tea, *roti-sabji*, etc.
22	Rice, *dal*, *sabji*, etc.

according to the taste and preference of the customers. A similar traditional relish in Assam is the *mahkarai* prepared out of a variety of lentil (*matimah*), bengal gram, rice, sesame all of which are parched.

Chanachur is a humbler kind of relish popular almost all over India. It is difficult to pinpoint its origin to any part of the country. However, as the main ingredient of the *chanachur* is *chana* (gram), its origin should be in a gram growing area of the country. From that point of view and also because nearly a large number of *chana* vendors hail from Bihar, it can be said that the origin of *chanachur* is in Bihar.

There are two types of *chana* vendors. One which vends from a box, on an elongated, cylindrical cane stand. They are widely prevalent and are very mobile. They have a fixed route which involves a few routine stops near schools, colleges, offices, cinema halls, etc. In the evening, they usually gravitate towards market places or children's parks. In addition to making these fixed rounds, a *chana* vendor takes advantage of any demand that may be created in a parking area particularly of trucks, taxis and rickshaws or near bus stands, city bus stops, and petrol filling stations or even in a railway crossing where vehicular traffic and people may halt momentarily.

The second type of chana vendors is less mobile. They push a heavy cart which is glass covered (Plate 3). They also follow a fixed route with one or two regular stops. The selling of this relish either from a box or a cart is a male province. These vendors all belong to the Bihari community and constitute the largest group of street food vendors (Fig. 5).

Vendors usually serve with the hand on squares of paper which are deftly turned into cones. As already mentioned, *chanachur* is a humbler kind of relish and can be eaten cheaply. One helping of this relish costs Rs. 0.50. It is very popular among people of Bihari, Punjabi and Marwari communities, students particularly girls and among people having a low income (Plates 4 and 5). Now a days *chanawalas* are also found near wine shops particularly in the evenings.

Phuska (small wheat dough puffs filled with a sour, peppery liquid) : These are small dough puffs prepared from wheat flour which are deep fried in oil. *Phuska* is also known as *gol gappa* or *pani puri.* It is eaten with a mixture of mashed potatoes and chick peas along with spicy tamarind water.

There are two kinds of *phuska* vendors. The first kind carries a *dala* which is a circular bamboo wicker basket with a wooden or cane stand (Plate 6). The second type, who are more mobile, push a small hand cart (Plate 7). *Phuskas* are usually vended near markets, parks, cinema halls, etc., in the afternoons and evenings from about 4 p.m. till about 9 p.m. However, vendors selling from push carts move about the whole day along definite routes. As a customer approaches the vendor, he is offered a conical paper bowl. One by one, the vendor starts serving the *phuskas*. The vendor punches the puffed top of the *phuska* with the thumb and stuffs it with a little bit of the potato mix and fills it with the spicy tamarind water. The whole dough puff along with the stuffing and the liquid is put in the mouth. Usually, three *phuskas* are served for Rs. 2.00 only. It has been observed that *phuska* eaters are not satisfied with eating only three. They keep on eating more till the need for it subsides.

Phuska is usually eaten by people belonging to the Marwari, Punjabi and Bihari communities and occasionally by the Assamese and the Bengalis. Since it is a relish eaten rarely out of compulsions of hunger, it is not a common food for the wage labourers.

Bhelpuri (a sweet and sour mixture of dough crisps, puffed rice etc.): It is a sweet and sour snack popularly associated with the city of Bombay, now renamed as Mumbai in Maharashtra, India. This snack has diffused from its home locale and has gained immense popularity all over India. *Bhelpuri* has become synonymous with the name of the city so much so that *bhelpuri* sold in places other than Mumbai is referred to as "Bombay *bhelpuri"*. It is unthinkable for a tourist or a visitor to Mumbai not to have tasted this relish. Even Hindi film songs sing of its tantalizing flavour and taste.

Bhelpuri is prepared from crushed dough crisps which are mixed with chopped onions, green chillies, sour and sweet chutney of tamarind and jaggery, puffed rice, boiled potatoes, sprouted green grams (optional) and coriander leaves.

The vendors of this food sell from tin boxes with collapsible lid. Inside the box, there are several compartments to store the ingredients of the *bhelpuri*. They are served on leaf, packets or paper plates and eaten with wooden spoons. The price for one such plate of *bhelpuri* costs Rs. 2.00 to Rs. 4.00. *Bhelpuris* are also sold from smaller push carts. All sellers of this food in the sample are from Bihar.

Jhalmuri (spicy puffed rice) : It is a spicy preparation made by mixing muri (puffed rice) with a variety of spices like red chilli powder, pepper powder, chopped green chillies, onions, fresh coriander leaves, grated raw papayas, boiled potatoes, etc., to which are added a few drops of lemon juice, tamarind chutney or jira pani (sour, spicy liquid).

The term *jhalmuri* is derived from the Bengali words *jhal* meaning spicy and hot and *muri* meaning puffed rice. Any food or relish prepared from *muri* or *cira* as the basic ingredient indicates a home root in eastern part of India, a rice growing area, somewhere in Bengal or Assam. This relish is very popular all over rural Bengal. However, it is important to mention that though this relish is indigenous to rural Bengal, all *jhalmuri* sellers in Guwahati are from Bihar (Fig. 5). *Jhalmuri* is sold in Guwahati from three kinds of devices. The first is a tin box measuring approximately

18 by 18 inches with a glass front. It is carried on one shoulder by the roving vendors. Second type is also a tin box similar to a *bhelpuri* seller's box. The third type uses a small push cart.

Jhalmuri is a relish that can be had cheaply at any time of the day. One serving of such a relish costs only ₹ 1.00. It is served on squares of paper or paper plates to be eaten with either a wooden spoon or with small pieces of paper.

Mumphali (ground nuts): *Mumphali* or *badam* is a very popular relish primarily eaten during the winter season. It is sold in different forms - roasted, fried and used as an ingredient of *chanachur.* They are sold by both mobile and stationary vendors from boxes, push carts and by squatting on the roadside. These vendors are by and large from Bihar (17) except a few (6) who are Bengalis. Generally, this trade is carried out by men. Occasionally, women vendors may also be seen. In this study, out of a total of 14 women vendors, 2 are groundnut sellers.

Along with the sale of groundnuts, many vendors particularly those selling from push carts also sell popcorn. Groundnuts are sold for ₹ 3.00 per 100 grams and popcorns for ₹ 1.00 per packet.

Makkai (roasted corn) : Like groundnuts, *makkai* is another popular winter relish. These are seen in street corners, bus stops, near market places, etc., where the vendors squat on the ground roasting corn over a makeshift charcoal fire. These vendors are mostly Bihari women who, after completing their domestic chores, sell this relish from about 4 p.m. till about 8 p.m. in the evening. Tender corn cobs are roasted over burning embers and are served hot with salt and lime rubbed over it to give a special flavour. Roasted corns are sold for ₹ 3.00 to ₹ 5.00, depending upon the size of the corn.

Snacks and light meals

This constitutes the second category of street food. These are not inherently street food but situation demands that they become so. Some of these snacks and light meals are typically sold in restaurants and snack bars. It ranges from slight snacks to light meals which are often eaten between the two main meals of the day. However, it is to be noted that the concept of 'snacks' and 'meals' vary in different social context and among different communities. Thus, it is important to distinguish between the two.

The people in nearly all parts of India make a clear distinction between a meal and a snack. Even the language reflects this difference. Many Indian languages like Assamese, Gujrati, Kannada, Tamil, to name a few, have separate verbs to differentiate between the two (Katona-Apte 1975:316). Snacking or nibbling, like in the West, is not done in India. But snacks which are prepared from grains, legumes, sugar and salt are often eaten along with tea or coffee between the two main meals of the day. Also, the use of a staple and its method of preparation determine whether a food is a snack or a meal. For instance, rice is the staple food in southern and eastern India. When rice grains are boiled whole and served with at least one side dish, it is considered a meal. Broken rice, powdered rice, flattened rice, puffed rice, fermented rice, etc., are considered as snack or tiffin in southern India and *jalpan* in Assam and Bihar. In northern India, where wheat is the staple food, all wheat preparations that are not unleavened bread are snacks, e.g., semolina, farina, cookies and other items prepared from wheat flour.

Sometimes a snack can be more substantial than a meal. It depends upon several factors such as the quality and quantity of the food offered, the eating habits of the individual and the socio-cultural background of the eater.

Some of the snacks and light meals commonly sold by street food sellers in Guwahati are discussed below.

Pakora (fritters): The fritters are fried pulse batter often containing vegetables, fish or meat. It is difficult to pinpoint the home locale of this snack because of its immense popularity and presence all over the country. It is known by various names such as *bara* (*vada*) in South India, *pakauri (pakoda)* in Bihar and Uttar Pradesh, *bor, phulori* and *pakora (pokori)* in Assam.

The *pakora* is usually prepared from a batter of *besan* (chick pea flour) and pulse paste to which is added chopped onions, green chillies, coriander leaves, salt, turmeric, etc. Small balls of this mixture are deep fried in hot oil. *Pakoras* are sold by stationary vendors from shops, stalls and push carts. During winter, particularly in the evenings, *pakora* sellers are seen making brisk business. Besides eating in the place of sale, customers pack hot fritters to be eaten at home.

In Guwahati, there are some very old and popular *pakora* vendors from where people even from a distance come to buy. They are located in Uzanbazar, Guwahati club area and near Assam Bengal Carriers (ABC) on the G.S. Road (Fig. 6). However, one of the earliest *pakora* sellers was an Assamese *paan* (betel nut and betel leaves) shop keeper located in Panbazar

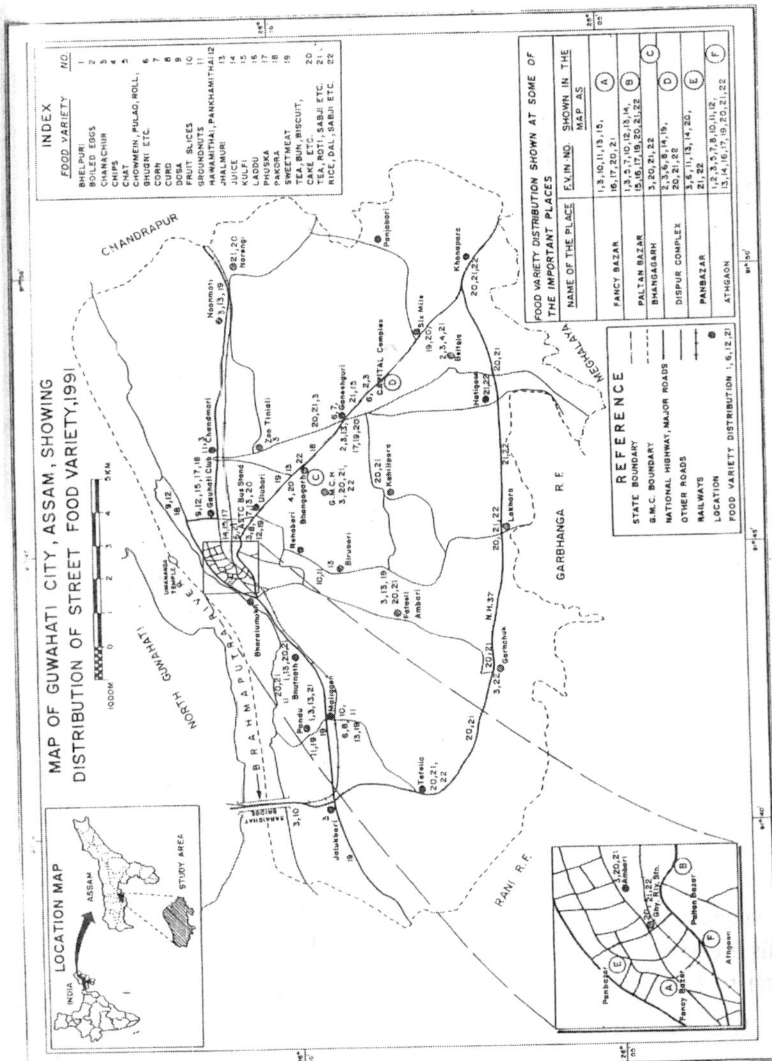
MAP OF GUWAHATI CITY, ASSAM, SHOWING
DISTRIBUTION OF STREET FOOD VARIETY,1991
LOCATION MAP
INDIA
ASSAM
STUDY AREA
INDEX
FOOD VARIETY NO.
BHELPURI 1
BOILED EGGS 2
CHANACHUR 3
CHIPS 4
CHAT 5
CHOWMEIN, PULAO, ROLL, GHUGNI ETC. 6
CORN 7
CURD 8
DOSA 9
FRUIT SLICES 10
GROUNDNUTS 11
HAWAMITHAI, PANKHAMITHAI 12
JHALMURI 13
JUICE 14
KULFI 15
LADDU 16
PHUSKA 17
PAKORA 18
SWEETMEAT 19
TEA, BUN, BISCUIT, CAKE ETC. 20
TEA, ROTI, SABJI ETC. 21
RICE, DAL, SABJI ETC. 22
REFERENCE
STATE BOUNDARY
G.M.C. BOUNDARY
NATIONAL HIGHWAY, MAJOR ROADS
OTHER ROADS
RAILWAYS
LOCATION
FOOD VARIETY DISTRIBUTION 1, 6, 12, 21
FOOD VARIETY DISTRIBUTION SHOWN AT SOME OF THE IMPORTANT PLACES
NAME OF THE PLACE | F.V. IN NO. | SHOWN IN THE MAP AS
FANCY BAZAR | 1,3,10,11,13,15, 16,17,20,21 | A
PALTAN BAZAR | 1,3,5,7,10,12,13,14, 15,16,17,19,20,21,22 | B
BHANGAGARH | 3,20,21,22 | C
DISPUR COMPLEX | 2,3,6,8,14,19, 20,21,22 | D
PANBAZAR | 3,6,11,13,14,20, 21,22 | E
ATHGAON | 1,2,3,5,7,8,10,11,12, 13,14,16,17,19,20,21,22 | F
BRAHMAPUTRA RIVER
NORTH GUWAHATI
CHANDRAPUR
MEGHALAYA
GARBHANGA R.F.
RANI R.F.
N.H.37
1000M 0 1 2 3 4 5KM

area of the city. This shop no longer exists, but earlier it was the only outlet of cooked food on the roadside in Guwahati.

Ranjit Kumar Sharma (63), a city based businessman, recalls his college days when he was a student of Cotton College from late 1940s to early 1950s. During those days there were very few restaurants in Guwahati. Three of the most popular were - Delight, Oasis and Ananda Jalpan. Besides these eating houses which sold chops, cutlets, omlettes, *bundiya-bhujia* (a sweet-salty mixture) and samosa/*singaras* (deep fried wheat patties with savoury stuffings), there was one other place which sold *pakoras*. It was a small shack on the roadside in Panbazar. It was run by a *paan* shop owner, who in the evening prepared fish, prawn and vegetable fritters. This place became so popular that a large crowd of customers used to gather every evening. They were served hot *pakoras* on pieces of paper. Many of them also packed and carry them home.

Nimki (salted, triangular dough crisps): It is a deep fried, salty, crisp triangular shaped snack prepared from wheat flour. The *nimki* cannot be localized to any particular area of India but found all over northern, western and eastern India. It is prepared from a dough made of wheat flour, vegetable oil, salt and water. Small balls of this dough are rolled and cut into halves. Each half is folded to form triangles which are deep fried in oil till light brown.

Nimkis are sold by stationary food vendors and often eaten along with tea. They are priced at ₹ 0.50 per piece. Along with the sale of *nimki*, many vendors sell *khurma*. It is a rectangular sweet snack of wheat flour and eaten along with tea. It is also priced at ₹ 0.50 per piece.

Laddu (sweet balls) : *Laddus* are sweet balls prepared from a variety of ingredients like *besan, cira, muri*, coconut, etc. They do not have a fixed home locale but are popular all over India. In Guwahati, *laddus* prepared from *cira, muri* and coconut are popular.

Cira and *muri laddu* are prepared by heating *gur*-to a honey like consistency and after it cools, parched *cira* and *muri* are added to it and balls are prepared. Coconut *laddu* and its preparation have already been described earlier[3].

The sellers of this snack are highly mobile. They belong to the Bihari community except for a few Bengali sellers who sell coconut *laddu*. There are no Assamese vendors selling *laddu*, though coconut *laddu* is an indigenous snack of the Assamese people.

The *laddu* vendors carry these items in tin boxes. They also carry a bell or a *dambaru* (small hand drum) to attract customers. *Laddus* are cheap and easily affordable. They are priced at Rs. 0.50 to Rs. 1.00 per *ladddu.* These sellers are frequently seen in the localities with mixed population comprising of Punjabis, Bihari, Bengali, Marwari, etc. This snack item can be consumed at any time of the day.

Malpua (a sweet snack of wheat and sugar syrup) : Traditionally, the *malpua* belongs to Jiaganj in Murshidabad district-of West Bengal. The basic ingredients of this sweet are *chhana* (Indian cottage cheese), *suji* (semolina) and *maida* (refined flour). It is prepared by mixing the above ingredients with a little water and forming small balls and given an elongated shape. It is fried in oil and boiled in hard sugar syrup to give it a brownish colour.

In Guwahati, *malpua* is prepared in a simple manner by mixing *maida* and water with a pinch of bicarbonate of soda. This mixture is beaten to a flowing consistency. Then a ladleful of the mixture is poured in a griddle of hot oil and fried. After removing from fire it is directly put into the sugar syrup and later removed.

Ghugni (chick pea curry) : It is a food popular in Bihar, parts of northern India, Rajasthan and Gujarat. It is eaten alone or along with *bhatura* (fried, leavened bread) or *roti* (unleavened bread). *Ghugni* or *chole* is a curry prepared by soaking and boiling *kabuli chana* (chick peas). When it becomes soft after boiling it is seasoned and fried in oil with the addition of spices like turmeric, cumin seeds, black pepper, salt, etc. *Ghugni* is sold by the stationary vendors and are priced at ₹ 2.00 per plate. The *bhaturas* cost ₹ 1.00 each.

Chaat (spicy, tangy, mashed potatoes) : This snack is a preparation of boiled, mashed potatoes. It is generally eaten with a fresh salad of tomato, onion, radish, carrot, etc., and garnished with boiled chick peas, tomato sauce or a tamarind and date chutney along with fresh coriander leaves and chillies (Plate 14). *Chaat* is sold by vendors primarily belonging to the Bihari community. It is priced at ₹ 2.00 per plate.

Chop : It is a salted food item which is either round or egg-shaped made from boiled potatoes. To most western readers chop would usually mean a thick slice of meat, especially pork or lamb including the rib. The chop of the West has been highly nativised in India and closely associated with the 'tea-cabin' culture in the urban milieu.

Chop is prepared by mashing boiled potatoes, to which is added salt, turmeric, coriander leaves and stuffed with fried vegetables or minced meat. It is deep fried in oil. Chops are also made by sandwiching two slices of bread with a layer of mashed potatoes. It is called bread chop or bread pakora. Sometimes chops are also prepared from boiled eggs. Chops are sold by vendors from shops, shacks or push carts (which are stationary) along with other items like tea, pakora, ghugni, etc. The chop, bread chop and egg chops are priced at ₹ 1.50, 1.00 and ₹ 2.00 respectively.

This snack is a favourite food for those who frequent restaurants and fast food stalls like college students, office-goers, etc. However, this same snack is available at a cheaper rate in the roadside stalls and commonly eaten by them. Rickshaw pullers and other informal sector workers do not usually eat chops, but bread chop which is cheaper and also filling is frequently eaten by them.

Roll : Unlike the concept of roll in the West which is a loaf of bread cut open and stuffed with a specific food - a sausage etc., the roll as sold by street food vendors in Guwahati is entirely different. It is prepared by rolling a roti (unleavened bread) with shredded and fried vegetables or meat usually mutton or chicken. It is sealed in the lower end with a sheet of paper so that the stuffing do not come out while eating.

Roll is prepared by stationary vendors belonging to Assamese and Bengali communities. This snack is sold by very few vendors (5) along with chowmein, pulao, chop, etc. The price of roll ranges from ₹ 4.00 to 8.00.

Chowmein (boiled and fried noodles) : It is basically a Chinese dish prepared by boiling noodles and adding boiled and fried vegetables to it. Sometimes eggs and shredded meat are added. Chowmein is a full meal in itself and can be eaten as a snack also. College students, office goers and casual shoppers generally eat chowmein (Plate 15). Hence, the sellers of this food are mostly seen near colleges and commercial areas.

Until a few years ago, chowmein was confined to restaurants. However, the fact that it can be cooked in less time and that a substantial quantity can be eaten cheaply has increased its popularity, thereby making its entry into street food arena very easy. The price of one full plate of vegetable chowmein is ₹ 8.00. This plate is about the size of a dinner plate and is served with a heapful of noodles which can be easily shared by two individuals. A similar plate of chicken noodles costs ₹ 12.00 to ₹ 15.00 only. The vendors of chowmein are generally Assamese and Bengali people who sell such food along with pulao, roll, chops, etc. from covered stationary push carts. There are 5 such sellers (Fig. 5). One of them used to sell from a motorized vehicle but is presently a restaurant owner.

Pulao (a rice dish) : It is a rice preparation of Central Asian origin and considered a delicacy. It is a course in its own right when cooked with vegetables or meat. The pulao was introduced into India by the Moghuls and became the main preparation in the Muslim cuisine in India (Chowdhury 1990).

Pulao is prepared from a fine, fragrant and long grained variety of rice. There are different methods of preparing pulao. In Guwahati, it is commonly prepared by cooking the rice grains partially and frying it with the addition of spices like onions, ginger, garlic, cumin seeds, salt, turmeric powder, bay leaves, etc. Pulao is usually eaten along with a vegetable or a meat curry either as a meal or as a substitute for meals. Pulao is sold by stationary sellers who sell chowmein, roll, chop, ghugni, roti-sabji, etc., and is priced between ₹ 5.00 to 10.00 per plate. The sellers of this food are not many in Guwahati (Fig. 5).

Dosa (rice and lentil pancakes) : It is typically a dish of the southern part of India, particularly in the states of Karnataka and Tamilnadu.

To prepare *dosa*, rice and a variety of lentil (urad) are ground in a definite proportion and mixed with little water to form a batter. A ladleful of this batter is poured over a flat pan or griddle to form a paper thin pancake. A stuffing of spiced potato mash, seasoned with salt, mustard seeds and spilt gram lentils are put in the pancake and folded lightly. The *dosa* is served hot along with *sambar* (a spicy lentil soup preparation) and a chutney. It can also be eaten without the stuffing, in which case it is called the paper *dosa* or plain *dosa* and can be eaten as a snack or as a substitute for a meal.

The *dosa* is no longer concentrated in its traditional home locale. It has diffused to distant areas and even acquired local flavours. It is a very popular food served in almost all good hotels and restaurants all over the country. Nowadays, in Guwahati, the *dosa* is also vended by mobile vendors. It is interesting to mention that the only dosa vendor in Guwahati, is not from south India but from Bihar.

Ratan Jha (22) is a Bihari dosa seller originally hailing from Champaran district of Bihar. He migrated to Guwahati following his elder brother who came prior to him. Ratan worked along with his brother in a small restaurant in Guwahati for about seven months. There he learnt how to prepare different types of food including the *dosa.*

During his stay in the restaurant, he had seen the immense popularity of *dosa* among people of different communities. It struck upon him that if he could sell quality *dosa* and provide it hot in the doorstep of the customers, he could make good business. So, he along with his brother (who still works in the restaurant) prepares the *dosa* mix at home. With the help of a licensed push cart he sells *dosa* from street to street in residential and business areas of the city.

Every day of the week from about 3 p.m. onwards till about 7 p.m., he prepares and sells *dosa* instantly from a hearth that he carries on the cart. On an average, he sells about 60 *dosas* per day at the rate of ₹ 4.00 per *dosa* (restaurant price ranges from ₹ 8.00 to ₹ 15.00 per *dosa*).

Bhapa pitha (steamed rice cake) : This snack is prepared from rice powder which is mixed with jaggery and water. It is given a circular shape and steamed. The *Bhapa pitha* is similar to the Assamese *tekeli mukhat diya pitha*. It is prepared by the Bihari vendors and eaten by the immigrant Muslim and Bihari rickshaw pullers, thela pullers and daily wage labourers. This cake is priced at ₹ 0.50 for a small sized one and ₹ 1.00 for a big one. It can also be eaten along with milk, in which case the price is ₹ 1.50. Since this food is very cheap and gives the feeling of fullness, it is a common snack among the daily workers.

Anda (egg) : Since the advent of modern methods of egg farming in India, 'vegetarian' or unfertilized eggs are slowly being accepted and eaten by Indian vegetarians. The egg, besides being a rich source of protein is also cheaply available. In the recent past, there has been a sudden proliferation in the egg supply to the city of Guwahati. This is primarily due to an increase in production at hatcheries in Andhra Pradesh from where large quantities of eggs are brought to Assam. Due to its increased supply, it began to be easily accessible at bus stops, market places and street corners in a boiled form. Street food vendors sit in convenient corners and offer boiled eggs along with salt. The egg, being a cheap source of protein is eaten by a large number of people belonging to the low socio-economic section and office workers, etc. However, it is not popular among Bihari rickshaw and thela pullers. Sale of boiled eggs is more in the evenings and during the winter season.

Sweetmeats

The third category of street food is comprised of sweetmeats. Sweets have always enjoyed a place of pre-eminence in the Hindu food categorization. In spite of sweetmeats being subjected to cooking (fried, baked, boiled, etc.) they are free from ritual pollution (Cantlie 1984:193). Due to this feature, sweetmeats have always been transported, sold in sweetmeat shops and weekly markets and also have gained easy entry into street food. However, all sweetmeats have not become street sweets. Only those sweetmeats which are portable as well as popular and also retain for sometime have found their way to the streets. In Guwahati, there are a number of street food vendors selling sweetmeats (Fig. 5). They are mainly two types. The first type are the stationary vendors who sell sweetmeats along with tea, bun, etc., from pushcarts, shops and stalls. The second type are the mobile vendors like the seasonal migrant Bengali sellers who come from Barddhaman district of West Bengal. These people who possess considerable skill in making sweetmeat come to Guwahati every year in search of a lucrative market and sell sweetmeats typical of their region. They sell mihidana and sitabhog. They prefer to sell in the streets in both residential and business areas, not because people look to the street to 'eat sweetmeat but to avoid any permanent establishment cost that a shop would incur.

There is also another group of roving sweetmeat sellers who do not prepare the sweets themselves but buy these from small manufacturers and sell them from door-to-door in different localities of the city. They are usually Bihari men who sell sandesh and sohnpapri. Some of the popular sweetmeats sold in the streets of Guwahati are described below.

Rasogolla (sweetmeat ball in syrup) : It is a very popular sweetmeat having its origin in West Bengal. Rasogolla is made from ingredients like chhana, suji, sugar and water. It is prepared by mixing *chhana* and *suji* thoroughly. The dough is divided into small portions rolled into balls. They are then cooked for about five minutes in boiling sugar syrup, after which they are transferred to a stock syrup which is thicker in consistency than the boiling syrup.

Rasogolla is one of the earliest sweetmeats to have been sold in Guwahati. Kamala Devi (81) is a resident of Bharalumukh, in Guwahati. She recalls that just after World War II and around the time of India's independence in 1947, itinerant sweetmeat sellers (mostly Bengali) used to sell rasogolla and curd from house to house. They used to balance two saucepans on either side carrying the sweetmeat and above this on a wooden board a clay bowl of curd. These Bengali vendors used to come twice a week. Her husband, who was very fond of sweets used to buy rasogollas regularly.

Today however, such sweet vendors are rare except in the Bengali populated areas of the city like Pandu, Maligaon, Rehabari, Noonmati Railway colony, etc. (Fig. 6).

Sandesh (sweetmeat of baked chhana and sugar) : It is a famous sweetmeat of West Bengal. The Bengali word sandesh originally meant "news"[4]. But with its long use it has primarily come to mean the sweetmeat itself. The basic ingredients used in the preparation of this sweet are chhana and a fine variety of sugar.

Sandesh is prepared by two methods. The first is by the addition of powdered sugar to the chhana which are mixed and cooked over a slow fire. After it cools, it is cast in different moulds to give a variety of shapes. The second method involves the use of syrup instead of powdered sugar. The rest of the process is similar to the first method. Sandesh is also prepared from jaggery, which is substituted for sugar. It is sold in Guwahati by Bengali and Bihari vendors.

Sohnpapri (light, fluffy sweetmeat) : Sohnpapri is a sweetmeat famous in parts of Bihar and Rajasthan. It is prepared from refined wheat flour, gram flour, clarified butter and sugar. All these ingredients are mixed in a definite proportion and fried over a medium fire for about two hours. After the mixture becomes liquid, it is removed from fire and ghee is added to it and allowed to cool. This is known as khurara. Then a syrup of sugar is prepared by heating sugar and a little proportion of unrefined sugar. When it becomes hard, it is removed from fire and the khurara is added to this syrup till it absorbs all of it. It is then slightly kneaded and spread over a wooden plank to be cut into squares.

In Guwahati, the sellers of Sohnpapri are primarily from Bihar and West Bengal. It is vended from tin boxes like those of the jhalmuri sellers and from saucepans.

Mihidana (fine sweet fritters) : It is a famous sweetmeat having its home locale in the Barddhaman district of West Bengal. These are fine, yellow coloured globules of pulse flour, fried in ghee, treated with sugar syrup and stored dry. The basic ingredients necessary are matar meal (peas pulse), kalai pulse (a variety of pulse), sugar, rice powder and ghee. A batter of the pulses are made after grinding it to a fine paste. A skimmer (with fine holes) is held over a hot pan of ghee. A cupful of the batter is put on the skimmer and tiny fritters rain down to the hot ghee. After straining they are put in the sugar syrup. When all of the fritters soak up the syrup they are transferred to a platter.

Mihidana is primarily sold by the seasonal migrant vendors from Barddhaman district of West Bengal. They carry with them sufficient quantities of dry mihidana and after coming to Guwahati, they soak these dry fritters in sugar syrup as and when necessary. These migrant vendors occasionally sell sitabhog (a sweetmeat resembling rice grains) along with mihidana.

Jilebi (coiled, tubular, fried pastry, soaked in sugar syrup) : It is a flat spiral of fermented batter, fried in hot oil and soaked hot in sugar syrup of medium consistency and removed. The jilebi finds mention in several ancient works[5].

It is prepared from a fermented mixture of refined flour, sugar, oil and rice flour. This mixture is fried over a pan of hot oil from a special device, usually a tumbler with a hole at the bottom. The batter filled tumbler is held over the pan and in a circular motion the hole is released. Crisp jilebis are strained and immediately put in the syrup.

Jilebis are sold in Guwahati by stationary vendors who sell pakoras. During festive occasions, this sweet is sold along with bundiya (sweet fritters), khurma, etc.

Beside the sweetmeats already described, there are a number of sweet items which are largely meant for children. They include hawa mithai, pankha mithai, chips, etc.

Hawa mithai (air-filled sweet) : It is a popular children's sweet resembling a ball of cotton wool. It is pink or yellow in colour and derives its name from the Hindi words hawa, meaning air, and mithai - a sweetmeat. It is so called because as one bites into this small ball of sweetmeat, air trapped inside comes out.

Hawa mithai is prepared in the same manner as sohnpapri except that it is made more fine and into small balls of spun sugar. This sweet is sold in polythene packets. Each packet contains six hawa mithais and priced at Rs. 1.00 only. The sellers, totaling nine, are all males from Bihar and are mobile. These vendors carry the packets by stringing them in a wire ring. Hawa mithai is also sold along with pankha mithai and sohnpapri in tin boxes.

Pankha mithai (fan-shaped sweet) : It is prepared from sugar solids and gets its name from its shape. It resembles a pankha (a Hindi word meaning hand-fan). This sweet is white in colour and striped with red and green colours. They are sold by the mobile vendors who are from Bihar. Like the hawa mithai, pankha mithai is also a children's sweet and is priced at ₹ 0.25 each.

Kulfi (a frozen dessert) : It is a frozen confection developed in India long before ice cream was manufactured commercially'. Brought by the Moghuls from Kabul or prepared by them in India, the *kulfi* derives its name from the conical metal device in which it was made. In the Ain-i-Akbari (1590 A.D.), the mode of preparation of *kulfi* finds place in the description of Emperor Akbar's royal kitchen. To prepare this dessert, a sweetened mixture of *khoa* (thickened milk, almost solid), dry fruits like pistachio, currants, and saffron strands are frozen in conical metal containers after sealing the contents with dough. These containers are put inside a *handi* (big clay pot) along with ice and salt and churned or rocked with both hands till the *kulfi* freezes.

The technique of making this ice cream is a very old one. *Kulfi* is also one of the oldest street food sold in Assam as well as in Guwahati. Today, the *kulfi* sellers (Bihari) are few in number and their market has increasingly been captured by machine made and industrially prepared ice creams and ice sticks. *Kulfi* is sold from carts for ₹ 1.00 each and the sellers are highly mobile.

Fruits and Fruit Juices

Selling of fruits on the roadside or on the pavements is a common activity in Guwahati. Fruit vendors sell variety of fruits like apple, banana, pineapple, mosambi, orange, pomegranate, grape, etc. But these do not constitute a part of street food. Such fruits are not prepared or sold in a ready-to-eat form. However, certain fruits like *anaras* (pineapple), *tarbuj* (watermelon), *narial* (coconut), *papita* (papaya), and *khira* (cucumber) are sold by street food vendors in a ready-to-eat and prepared manner. These fruits are cut into sections and displayed on tray, dish or boxes and sold by mobile vendors (Plate 21). All vendors selling fruits belong to the Bihari community and predominantly males. There are many street food vendors who take to the selling of seasonal fruits at one time of the year alternately with the sale of *chanachur* or *jhalmuri*, etc.

Besides the eating of seasonal fruits in the streets, drinking of juice, particularly in summer, is popular. *Ganne ka ras* (sugar cane juice), *dab* (tender coconut water) and coloured drinks are commonly available (Plates 22, 23 and 24). Sugar cane juice is sold by vendors from Bihar who are mobile. Tender coconut is sold exclusively by the Assamese vendors who are stationary.

Meals

The last category of street food is basically home food but because of urban compulsions and demand have come to the street. These are the meals which comprise of *roti* (unleavened bread) or *bhat* (boiled rice) as the staple food. These are eaten along with *dal* (lentils) and different types of curries, both vegetarian and non-vegetarian.

Roti-sabji : Meal prepared with *roti* as the principal food is the staple diet of most people from Bihar, Uttar Pradesh and parts of North India, etc. Dry roasted forms of *roti* include the common *chapati*, roasted on a hot griddle and sometimes puffed out to a *phulka* by brief contact with live coals. Sometimes, wheat dough after rolling out can be either pan fried using just a little fat or deep fried. The first kind is common and often round or triangular in shape. It is the *paratha*. The *roti* and the *paratha* are always eaten with a *sabji* (curry) commonly prepared from seasonal vegetables or *dal* (Plate 25).

A *roti-sabji* meal is sold by stationary sellers and consumed both as a snack as well as a meal. It is eaten by daily wage earners and other informal sector workers. In addition, office goers and travellers also form a significant group. This food besides being a filler is also cheap. It is priced at ₹ 0.50 per *roti* and ₹ 1.00 for a plate of curry.

Bhat (boiled rice) : The eating of rice is a part and parcel of the life of the people in eastern and southern India. In India, there are many ways of cooking rice. It may be boiled, steamed, fried or flavoured with different ingredients. However, the proper way to cook rice is a controversial subject because there are so many different methods of doing so6. In Assam, boiled rice is not only the staple food but is regarded as the only food upon which life is dependent. In the traditional Hindu context, the eating of boiled rice was carried out according to elaborate rules of ritual purity (Cantlie 1984 : 194). Boiled rice and all other dishes such as *dal, bhaji,* fish or meat curry were cooked in the kitchen. If they were cooked outside, the hearth, burnt ashes and all wastes of fire were thrown away. The rigidity associated with the preparation and eating of rice and its accompanying dishes was so high (in the Hindu context) it was unthinkable that boiled rice could emerge as a component of street food.

In Guwahati, stationary street food vendors provide both vegetarian and non-vegetarian meals. A vegetarian meal consists of boiled rice, *dal,* vegetable curry and fried vegetable preparation. A non-vegetarian meal consists of the above mentioned items and a curry which is of either fish or meat - usually goat's meat. However, pork and beef are also cooked in those areas where the demand for such meat exists7. For instance, pork is eaten by certain scheduled caste communities while beef is eaten by the Muslims (Plate 26).

The vendors who provide rice and curry meals are always of stationary nature and have some kind of sitting arrangements. They belong to Bihari, Bengali and Assamese communities and operate from shops, stalls or carts. These vendors are found in large numbers near the Guwahati railway station, Dispur Capital Complex, Guwahati Medical College Hospital, Adabari Bus Stand, near the Fancy Bazar wholesale market, rickshaw and *thela* stands and along the National Highway No. 37 by pass (Fig. 6). These vendors not only cater to the afternoon meals of a large number of transient and floating population in the city but also provide meals at night for those who have no cooking arrangement at their place of stay. It has been observed that stationary vendors who during the daytime sell tea, bun, biscuit, *chaat, pakora*, etc., switch over to meals at night for a host of permanent customers like daily wage earners, shopkeepers, *thela,* rickshaw pullers, pony cart operators, numerous other informal sector workers, bus and truck drivers, travellers and even office workers who have no families along with them. Though there are only 32 sellers of rice meals and 24 *roti-sabji* sellers, at night they and 18 sellers of tea, bun, biscuit, etc., take to the selling of meals making it the single largest category of street food to be sold in Guwahati. Thus, the popular misconception that street food are snacks and not real meals holds no ground.

A look at the varieties of street food discussed in this chapter shows that these are not indigenous food of the Assamese, but largely introduced and popularized by the migrants who came from other parts of the country. Assamese food inspite of having the attributes of street food such as portability, durability, etc., never appeared as street food. One can perhaps rationalize this from a historical point of view. Assamese people lacked a tradition of eating out. They were basically cultivators. Participation in trade and commerce was negligible. It was only gradually, after several groups of immigrant people began to settle in Assam and pressure on land began to mount, that Assamese people took to occupations other than cultivation. When some of them started street food vending the market was already taken up popular non-Assamese varieties of street food leaving no place for Assamese food.

Notes

1. For details, see Khare 1976a and 1976b, Achaya 1994:62-68.
2. Industrially manufactured juice, aerated drinks and ice creams have been left outside the purview of this study.
3. Please refer to Chapter Two, p. 31.
4. Whenever one has to enquire about the news of any relatives or friends, it was customary to send sweets along with the messenger.
5. For details, see Achaya 1994:155.
6. For details see Achaya 1994:33,34,35; Cantlie 1984:194-202 and Choudhury 1990.
7. See also Chapter Five, p. 91.

Chapter - 5

Street Food Vendors

Food vending in an important part of the modern life which serves two vital functions. First, it serves food quickly and cheaply to a large section of urban dwellers and visitors. Secondly, it provides employment to a number of people who do not have educational qualification or skill for urban employment. In Guwahati, selling of street food is a common sight. The street food vendors sell different items from temporary sheds, shops, pushcarts or by moving from locality to locality. They are seen near marketplaces, city bus stops, cinema halls and sometimes in street corners along busy thoroughfares in commercial, residential and office areas.

DEMOGRAPHIC OUTLINE OF STREET FOOD VENDORS

The sellers of street food in Guwahati are people who come from diverse regional, linguistic, religious, caste and socio-cultural background. They do not belong to one homogenous social group. The demographic profile of street food sellers in Guwahati based on data collected from a sample of 360 street food vendors within the municipal limits of Guwahati is outlined below.

Age, Sex and Marital Status

The population of food vendors along with age, sex and marital status are shown in table 1.

In Table 1, the age of street food vendors varies from 15 to 60 years and above. The highest numbers of vendors belong to the age group of 30 to 34 years. They constitute 24.72 per cent of the total number of vendors. Also, maximum numbers of vendors are concentrated in the age groups of 25 to 44 years. Thereafter the number of vendors decreases as the age increases. The median age of the street food vendors in Guwahati (including male and female) is 33.08 years.

Table 5.1. Distribution of Street Food Vendors According to Age, Sex and Marital Status

Age group	Marital status																Total population					
	Unmarried				Married				Widowed				Divorced/separated									
	M		F		M		F		M		F		M		F		M		F		T	
	No.	%	No.	%	No.	%	No.	%	No.	%	No.	%	No.	%	No.	%	No.	%	No.	%	No.	%
15-19	16	4.44	0	0.00	8	2.22	1	0.28	0	0.00	0	0.00	0	0.00	0	0.00	24	6.67	1	0.28	25	6.94
20-24	10	2.78	0	0.00	22	6.11	0	0.00	0	0.00	0	0.00	0	0.00	0	0.00	32	8.89	0	0.00	32	8.89
25-29	9	2.50	1	0.28	55	15.28	2	0.56	0	0.00	0	0.00	0	0.00	1	0.28	64	17.78	4	1.11	68	18.89
30-34	12	3.33	0	0.00	74	20.56	2	0.56	0	0.00	0	0.00	0	0.00	1	0.28	86	23.89	3	0.83	89	24.72
35-39	1	0.28	0	0.00	40	11.11	4	1.11	0	0.00	1	0.28	0	0.00	0	0.00	41	11.39	5	1.39	46	12.78
40-44	0	0.00	0	0.00	45	12.50	0	0.00	1	0.28	1	0.28	0	0.00	0	0.00	46	12.78	1	0.28	47	13.06
45-49	0	0.00	0	0.00	25	6.94	0	0.00	0	0.00	0	0.00	0	0.00	0	0.00	25	6.94	0	0.00	25	6.94
50-54	0	0.00	0	0.00	21	5.83	0	0.00	0	0.00	0	0.00	0	0.00	0	0.00	21	5.83	0	0.00	21	5.83
55-59	0	0.00	0	0.00	4	1.11	0	0.00	1	0.28	0	0.00	1	0.28	0	0.00	6	1.67	0	0.00	6	1.67
60+	0	0.00	0	0.00	1	0.28	0	0.00	0	0.00	0	0.00	0	0.00	0	0.00	1	0.28	0	0.00	1	0.28
Total	48	13.33	1	0.28	295	81.94	9	2.50	2	0.56	2	0.56	1	0.28	2	0.56	346	96.11	14	3.89	360	100.00

Table 1 also shows the sex composition of the population. The percentage of males is higher than the females. This is due to the fact that most of the vendors who come to the city for work are not accompanied by their womenfolk. Moreover, the vendors come from communities where certain vocations are essentially male centered. There are fourteen women vendors who are mostly of Bihari origin. They sell roasted peanuts, roasted maize and few of them also sell tea, snacks and meals.

Table 1 also gives the marital status of food vendors. The highest number of married vendors (76) are included in the age group of 30 to 34 years. From the group of unmarried vendors, 16 are too young to marry. Out of the total number of vendors only a few (7) are widowed, divorced or separated. This includes 4 females and 3 males.

Family Size and Composition

The families of street food vendors vary in numerical composition. Table 2 gives the distribution of families according to numerical size. There is a considerable range from 2 to 28 family members. The average size of a vendor's family is 6.75.

Table 5.2: Numerical Size of Street Food Vendor's Family

No. of persons/family	Families No.	%
1-3	36	11.01
4-6	175	53.52
7-9	60	18.35
10-12	31	9.48
13-15	10	3.06
16-18	7	2.14
19-21	4	1.22
22-24	3	0.92
25-27	0	0.00
28 & above	1	0.31
Total*	327	100.00

*It includes 6 husband-wife couples, 25 joint ventures between brothers and 1 venture between 2 brothers and a friend

Table 2 shows that 36 families have 1 to 3 members. The highest concentration, i.e., 175 families has 4 to 6 members and 60 families have members between 7 to 9. There are 31 families which have 10 to 12 members and 25 families with members ranging from 13 and above. There is only 1 family with 28 members. There is no family with 22 to 24 members.

The kin composition of street food vendors' families is given in Table 3. The range of composition of the families with regard to kinship is much wider than the range in numerical size.

Table 5.3: Kin Composition of Street Food Vendor's Family

Composition	*Families*	
	No.	*%*
Ego (E)*, wife (Wi)	29	8.87
E, Wi, Children (C)**	202	61.78
E, Wi, married son (mr- So), Sons' wives (o Wi), Sons' Children (So C)	7	2.14
E, Wi, C, widowed mother (Wd-Mo)	56	17.13
E, Wi, C, Wd- Mo, Unmarried Brother (Un- Br), Unmarried Sister (Un- Si)	6	1.83
E, Wi, C, Married Brothers (mr- Br), Brothers' wives (Br- Wi), Brothers children (Br- C)	1	0.31
E, Wi, C, Un-Br, U-Si	12	3.67
E, Un- Br	5	1.52
E, Co-wives	1	0.31
E (Widow), C	4	1.22
E (Widower), C	3	0.91
E, Wi, C, Father (Fa), Mother (Mo), Father's windowed sister (Fa-Wd-Si), Father' Sister's Son (Fa-Si-So), mr-Br, mr-Br-Wi, mr-Br-C	1	0.31
Total	327	100.00

* E (Ego) indicates the head of the household who is always a male unless otherwise indicated.
** Unmarried children.

It is evident from the table that the elementary family comprising of husband, wife and unmarried children predominates. It constitutes 61.78 per cent of the total sample. There are several variations of the nuclear family. It includes husband and wife family constituting 8.87 per cent. The second type is through inclusion of unmarried brothers and sisters to the nuclear family, which constitutes 17 families (5.28%). The third type consists of families with one of the spouse dead or separated. This category includes 7 families (2.14%). The rest are all joint families or its variations. There is only one case of polygyny from the entire study sample.

Levels of literacy and educational attainment

Educational attainment also varies across the sample. Table 4 shows levels of education by age and sex.

Table 5.4: Levels of Literacy and Educational attainment of street food vendors by age and sex

		Age Group										*Education Level*						
		Illiterate		Barely literate		*Primary School*		*Middle School*		*High School*		*Under Graduate*		*Graduate and above*		*Total*		
		M	F	M	F	M	F	M	F	M	F	M	F	M	F	M	F	T
15-19	No	10	1	4	0	0	0	5	0	5	0	0	0	0	0	24	1	25
	%	2.78	0.28	1.11	0.00	0.00	0.00	1.39	0.00	1.39	0.00	0.00	0.00	0.00	0.00	6.67	0.28	6.94
20-24	No	7	0	6	0	10	0	6	0	2	0	0	0	0	0	32	0	32
	%	1.94	0.00	1.67	0.00	2.78	0.00	1.67	0.00	0.56	0.00	0.00	0.00	0.00	0.00	8.89	0.00	8.89
25-29	No	18	1	7	0	25	0	10	1	4	2	0	0	0	0	64	4	68
	%	5.00	0.28	1.94	0.00	6.94	0.00	2.78	0.28	1.11	0.56	0.00	0.00	0.00	0.00	17.78	1.11	18.89
30-34	No	30	2	20	0	32	0	0	1	4	0	0	0	0	0	86	3	89
	%	8.33	0.56	5.56	0.00	8.89	0.00	0.00	0.28	1.11	0.00	0.00	0.00	0.00	0.00	23.89	0.83	24.72
35-59	No	51	3	37	2	36	1	12	0	3	0	0	0	1	0	140	6	146
	%	14.17	0.83	10.28	0.56	10.00	0.28	3.33	0.00	0.83	0.00	0.00	0.00	0.28	0.00	38.89	1.67	40.56
60& above	No	1	0	0	0	0	0	0	0	0	0	0	0	0	0	1	0	1
	%	0.28	0.00	0.00	0.00	0.00	0.00	0.00	0.00	0.00	0.00	0.00	0.00	0.00	0.00	0.28	0.00	0.28
Total	No	117	7	74	2	103	1	33	2	18	2	0	0	1	0	346	14	360
	%	32.50	1.94	20.56	0.56	28.61	0.28	9.17	0.56	5.00	0.56	0.00	0.00	0.28	0.00	96.11	3.89	100.00

In Table 4, out of a total of 360 vendors, 124 (34.4%) are illiterate and 76 vendors (21.1 %) are barely literate who can only sign their names. They have no formal schooling. From the vendors who have been to school, 104 (28.9%) have studied up to the primary level. Thirty five (9.7%) vendors have reached middle level school and 20 (5.5%) have studied till high school. This includes 5 vendors who have completed their high school education. There is only one person (0.27%) who has completed graduate level and there are no vendors with technical or non technical degree, diploma or certificates.

Women's education in the sample studied also reflects the same trend. From the total of fourteen female vendors, seven are illiterate, two can barely sign their names and the remaining five have crossed various levels of schooling. Two have even passed high school, making them eligible for a job in the minimum level in a government organization. In spite of this they have to take to street food vending.

In general, education appears to be at a very low level. Illiteracy, discontinued education and school dropouts are responsible for the poor standard of education among vendors.

Ram Kumar Yadav (17) is a school dropout from Chapra district of Bihar. He was a student of class VIII in a high school in the district. He had an argument with his class, teacher and in the process, Ram Kumar severely beat up his teacher. To escape his crime, he left his village and boarded a train to Assam. Here he came and stayed with a fellow villager (of the same caste) and took to the selling of ice creams on the street of Guwahati. Ice cream business being a seasonal one, he shifted to the selling of sweetmeats on a commission basis.

He said that he would have continued with his studies had the incident not taken place. Now he is in constant fear that police will come to catch him. So he wants to stay in Guwahati as long as possible.

From the foregoing discussion, it is clear that street food vendors are by and large illiterate. Secondly, most of the vendors who have been to school sometime in their life have forgotten the alphabets. This affects the day to day functioning of the vendors in the trade. With such a low level of education, getting job in the formal sector is unlikely. Often street food vendors have been accused of being young people waiting for jobs in formal sector thereby making this activity and the sector very transitory and peripheral. In the first place, vendors are not young but middle aged men and women. Secondly, low level of education cannot provide job in a country where unemployment is rampant. Under such conditions vendors have very little option but to stay in the informal sector which requires less education and skill.

Community affiliation

As indicated earlier, the vendors do not belong to one homogeneous social group. They are mainly comprised of people hailing from three states in the eastern region of the country, namely, Bihar, West Bengal and Assam. In terms of ethnic-linguistic categorization, they may be referred to as Bihari, Bengali, Assamese, etc. Table 5 gives the community wise distribution of street food vendors in Guwahati.

Table 5.5: Distribution of Street Food Vendors According to Community

Community		*Types of street food vendors*								
		Stationary			*Mobile*			*Total*		
		M	*F*	*T*	*M*	*F*	*T*	*M*	*F*	*T*
Bihari	No.	20	2	22	204	6	210	224	8	232
	%	5.56	0.56	6.11	56.67	1.67	58.33	62.22	2.22	64.44
Bengali	No.	21	3	24	46		46	67	3	70
	%	5.83	0.83	6.67	12.78	0.00	12.78	18.61	0.83	19.44
Assamese	No.	48	3	51	2		2	50	3	53
	%	13.33	0.83	14.17	0.56	0.00	0.56	13.89	0.83	14.72
Others	No.	3	3	2		2	5			5
	%	0.83	0.00	0.83	0.56	0.00	0.56	1.39	0.00	1.39
Total	No.	92	8	100	254	6	260	346	14	360
	%	25.56	2.22	27.78	70.56	1.67	72.22	96.11	3.89	100.00

It is evident from the table that majority of the vendors belong to the Bihari community (64.4%) followed by Bengalis (19.4%) and Assamese vendors (14.7%). It is clear that the largest section of vendors (85.3%) are non-Assamese as compared to the Assamese vendors who constitute only 14.7 per cent of the total. This is primarily due to the fact that participation of Assamese people in wage labour, trade and commerce in general is negligible[1]. The table also gives the distribution of vendors according to stationary and mobile form of vending. The Biharis who constitute the majority are mobile vendors. On the other hand, the Assamese vendors Operate from stationary makeshift arrangements. The category 'others' include 5 vendors of whom 3 are immigrants and 2 hailing from other states of the country. The types of food sold by Bihari vendors consist of relishes and snacks which are highly portable and move from place to place in search of customers. These foods are basically eaten on the street by standing.

Caste

A study of caste backgrounds of the street food vendors shows that people belonging to different castes having different hereditary occupations practise street food vending. Table 6 shows the caste of the street food vendors in Guwahati.

Table 5.6: Distribution of Street Food Vendors According to Caste/Community

Community	*Case*	*No.*	*%*
Bihari	Brahmin	20	5.56
	Bania	21	5.83
	Goyala	17	4.72
	Halwai	21	5.83
	Mallh	9	2.50
	Nonia	17	4.72
	Rajput	30	8.33
	Sonar	20	5.56
	Tatawa	27	7.50
	Teli	20	5.56
Bengali	Brahmin	8	2.22
	Baidya	15	4.17
	Moira	16	4.44
	Namasudra	10	2.78
	Suri	11	3.06
Assamese	Brahmin	2	0.56
	Haloi	10	2.78
	Hira	9	2.50
	Kalita	17	4.72
	Koch	4	1.11
	Keot	10	2.78
Others		46	12.78
Total		360	100.00

It is seen, from Table 6 that vendors coming from Bihar primarily belong to the following castes: Brahmins (priestly caste), Baniya (lending and mercantile business), Goyala (milk business), Halwai (sweet meat maker), Mallah (boatmen), Nonia (earth work), Rajput (warrior), Sonar (goldsmith), Tatawa (weavers) and Teli (oil pressers). From among them, Rajput and Tatawa castes show the highest concentration. Though, traditionally, they were not associated with cooking or vending of food, it can be assumed that their significant number among the street food vendors of Guwahati is the result of caste acting as a channel of communication for migration of people of their own caste groups to Guwahati.

Bengali vendors from West Bengal and Assam belong to the Brahmin (priestly caste), Baidya (traditional practitioners of medicine), Moira (sweetmeat makers and confectioners), Namasudra (fisherman) and Suri (maker of country liquor). In the study sample, none of the Bengali caste groups predominates.

The Assamese vendors primarily belong to the Brahmin (priestly caste), Kalita (agriculturist)[2], and a few belong to Haloi (ploughing), Hira (hand-made potter caste), Keot[3] and Koch[4]. From the Assamese castes, the Kalita caste shows the highest number of vendors.

The category 'others' constitute the highest number of vendors, accounting for 12.78 per cent. It includes 14 Muslim vendors and the rest from different Hindu caste groups and communities.

The association of caste with hereditary occupation is an important feature of the caste system in India. Most castes in addition to their traditional occupations also practise agriculture. Agriculture is by and large a caste free occupation. It should be noted that in the context of Assam, the occupational structure of caste has certain distinguishing features[5]. In the first place, the Assamese society is devoid of any rigidity with regard to caste based occupation. Secondly, the number of artisan castes is small. This is because many tasks, which in other parts of the country are done by particular castes, are carried out by individual households. Thirdly, the specialist castes that exist in Assam like Kumar (potters), Kamar (blacksmith), Jogi (silkworm rearers), Kaibarta (fishermen), etc., are not tied into a jajmani (patron-client) relation with land owning households. They sell their products within the village or in the market. Lastly, under the Vaishnavite influence brought about by Shri Sankardeva, the rigidity associated with caste hierarchy and untouchability has been brought down.

There is no specialist caste of cooks in the Indian or in the regional context of Assam. However, two caste groups, the Halwai of Bihar and Moira of West Bengal have been traditionally associated with sweetmeat making. The social standing of the Halwai is respectable. The reason as to why the Halwai caste occupied a good position perhaps resulted from the necessity that other castes should be able to take food from them. The *kacca* food (food cooked in water) could be eaten by the higher castes only near the hearth after it had been sufficiently cleansed and spread with cow dung. Also, the eater should be ritually pure to partake of such food. But the continuous need of businessmen to eat from out-of-home sources, where they cannot cook for themselves, has permitted them to eat food cooked without water or ghee, i.e., *pakka* food like sweetmeat and confectionery items. The Halwai, the maker of these items, has been given the position of a pure Caste from whose hands a member of the higher castes only near the hearth after it had been sufficiently cleansed and spread with cow dung. Also, the eater should be ritually pure to partake of such food. But the continues need of businessmen to eat from out-of-home sources, where they cannot cook for themselves, has permitted them to eat food cooked without water or ghee, i.e. *pakka* food like sweetmeat and confectionary items. The Halwai, the marker of these items, has been given the position of a pure case from whose hands a member of the higher castes can also accept water. The Moira caste of West Bengal is the equivalent of the Halwai caste of Bihar. They are also the sellers of sweetmeat.

Today, there has been a considerable change in the traditional occupation of the two caste groups (Sinha 1986:254). Those Halwais or Moiras whose income from traditional vocations have not been sufficient have adopted different professions, including street food vending.

Ram Vilas Sahu (53) hails from Buxar in Bihar and belongs to the sweetmeat making caste of Halwai. His family was involved with sweetmeat making for several generations. After the death of his father, he along with his four brothers took over the management of the family occupation. Due to some difference Of opinion regarding sharing of profit, he left the family business and came to Patna, the capital of Bihar, in search of a job. After a long search, he worked as a karigar (helper in a sweetmeat shop) for about two years. Not being satisfied with this job, he decided to open his own shop. But luck did not favour him. He decided to come to Assam because his distant uncle has been inviting him to come and join him in street food vending. Thus, he started by selling roil and sabji in a street stall along with his uncle in A.T. Road, Guwahati. He is of the opinion that food vending is an activity which does not require special skill and can be learned easily. Sahu has not forgotten the art of sweetmeat making because during festivals, particularly during Durga puja (autumn festival to propitiate Mother Goddess Durga), he makes different kinds of traditional sweets.

Bhanu Dutta (45) belongs to the Moira caste of West Bengal. He migrated to Guwahati from Barddhaman district of West Bengal some twelve years ago. His family used to have a small sweetmeat shop and some cultivable land. He left his natal place in search of job because their shop ceased to be profitable. Increased prices of milk and sugar, the need to modernize and innovate the sweetmeat shop, high competition and lack of skilled labour are some of the factors which made him leave his family calling and take to street food vending.

Table 5.7: Classification of Vendors According to Religion

Religion	Type of Vendors					
	Stationary		Mobile		Total	
	No.	%	No.	%	No.	%
Hindu	96	26.67	250	69.44	346	96.11
Islam	4	1.11	10	2.78	14	3.89
Others		---		---		---
Total	100	27.78	260	72.22	360	100.00

Religion

The vendors belong to two religious faiths. Table 7 shows the religious composition of the city's street food vendor population.

Table 7 shows that the majority of the vendors are Hindus. The other group of vendors belong to the Islamic religious faith. While vendors professing Hindu religion are distributed throughout the city, the Muslim vendors numbering fourteen are generally found in the areas where Muslim residents reside. This is only in case of sellers selling from stalls, shops and pushcarts. In Guwahati, there are as many as thirteen concentrations of Muslim people (Ali 1974:195). However, at present these have expanded and increased in number. Out of these, the concentration of Muslim population is high in Machkhowa and Lakhtokia. Besides these areas, Hedayatpur, Islampatty and Hatigaon are also worth mentioning.

The Muslim sellers belong to Bihari, Bengali and Assamese community. They sell different kinds of relishes, snacks, light meals and non- vegetarian meals consisting of beef.

Umar Ali (40) is a daily wage labourer who stays in a rented house in Hedayatpur. He is married with two children but they all live in their natal home in Hajo about 40 Kms west of Guwahati. Umar shares a room with two other daily wage labourers who are Muslims. They have no cooking arrangement in the house. So, they are solely dependent on the nearby street stall for their day-to-day food. The stall that Umar and his room mates visit is owned by a Bengali Muslim vendor who sells tea, bun, biscuit, cake in the morning and roti, sabji, rice and dal in the afternoons and evenings. In addition, twice a week, he prepares beef and mutton curry. Umar spends about ₹ 20.00 to 25.00 per day for food, including meals.

Besides Umar, there are several others like him who do not have a kitchen and eat their food cheaply from these street stalls. Not only people without a kitchen eat from roadside stalls but a few neighbouring Muslim households also carry home beef curry to be eaten with home cooked meals. They say that since they do not have to cook themselves and it is available cheaply, they prefer to buy from these nearby stalls.

Besides beef curry, Muslim vendors also sell special food during the Ramadan month[6].

Aslam Shah (46) is a street food vendor in Lakhtokia. He hails from Darbhanga district of Bihar. He has been selling tea, bun, biscuit, puri and sabji for several years in a corner of the busy market place of Lakhtokia. He is unmarried and lives in a rented room in the same locality not very far from his street food stall. In the place of sale, he gets a large number of customers during the day who are the casual shoppers, rickshaw and thela pullers and other vendors and hawkers. At night he has a number of permanent customers for whom he cooks meals. These are sellers who do not have their families with them. All these permanent customers are Muslims and live nearby. During the Ramadan month, the eating habits of the Muslim people are altered because of fasting during the day. Special type of food are prepared to break the fast after sundown and for eating during the night. This special food includes pulao, beef or mutton curry and *suji ka halwa* (a kind of sweet prepared from semolina). Aslam prepares this food for all Muslim customers who keep their fast and eat this special food together after sunset.

The above case is one instance where seasonality in street food varies with religion.

Language

The street food vendors of Guwahati are people who belong to different regions of the country and speak different languages and dialects. The food vendors mainly belong to three communities - Bihari, Bengali and Assamese. Each of these ethnic groups has their distinctive language and dialects. Table 8 classifies the vendors according to their mother tongue.

It is evident that majority of the vendors (85.3%), speak a language not native to Assam. The Bihari vendors who form the largest group speak either Bhojpuri, Maithili or Magahi.

Table 5.8: Distribution of Street Food Vendors According to Mother Tongue

Mother Tongue	*Vendors*	
	No.	*%*
Bhojpuri	80	22.2
Maithili	89	24.7
Magahi	63	17.5
Bengali	72	20.0
Assamese	53	14.7
Hindi	1	0.30
Marathi	1	0.30
Nepali	1	0.30
Total	360	100.00

Though the vendors covered in the study speak their distinctive mother tongue among themselves, for the purpose of day-to-day trading in street food they usually speak a language which is easily understood by the customers. Generally, Hindi, the national language, and a form of broken Assamese are spoken by the vendors.

MIGRATION OF STREET FOOD VENDORS

Migration indicates the movement of people from one place to another. It may be from within or outside the country, state, district or village. The street food vendors of Guwahati have migrated from different parts of the country primarily from Bihar, West Bengal and different parts of Assam. It is important to mention that Bihar and West Bengal are the neighbouring states of Assam and there is a long standing tradition of immigration of people from these areas since the inception of British colonial rule in Assam in the 1830s. People from these states have been coming in search of jobs and other economic opportunities. Table 9 classifies the vendors according to their place of birth.

From Table 9 it is evident that majority of the vendors were born within the country with the exception of three vendors who were born in Bangladesh (2) and Nepal (1). From those born in India, a large majority are non-Assamese, hailing from the states of Bihar and West Bengal. Out of 66 vendors born in Assam, 13 are Bengali vendors. The category 'others'.

Table 5.9: Distribution of Street food vendor according to place of Birth

Birth Place		*Type of vendors*					
		Stationary		*Mobile*		*Total*	
		No.	*%*	*No.*	*%*	*No.*	*%*
Total population	T	100	27.78	260	72.22	360	100
	R	94	26.11	255	70.83	349	96.94
	U	6	1.67	5	1.39	11	3.06
A Born in India	T	97	26.94	260	72.22	357	99.17
	R	91	25.28	255	70.83	346	96.11
	U	6	1.67	5	1.39	11	3.06
I Within the state of enumeration	T	64	17.78	2	0.56	66	18.33
	R	59	16.39	2	0.56	61	16.94
	U	5	1.39			5	1.39
(a) Born in the place of enumeration (i,e. Guwahati) (b) Elsewhere in the district of enumeration (i. e., Kamrup)	T	15	4.17			15	4.17
	R	15	4.17			15	4.17
	U						
(c) Born in other districts of the state	T	49	13.61	2	0.56	51	14.17
	R	44	12.22	2	0.56	46	12.78
	U	5	1.39			5	1.39
II. States in India beyond the state of enumeration	T	33	9.17	258	71.67	291	80.83
	R	32	8.89	253	70.28	285	79.17
	U	1	0.28	5	1.39	6	1.67
(a) Bihar	T	22	6.11	210	58.33	232	64.44
	R	21	5.83	206	57.22	227	63.06
	U	1	0.28	4	1.11	5	1.39
(b) West Bengal	T	19	5.28	38	10.56	57	15.83
	R	19	5.28	37	10.28	56	15.56
	U			1	0.28	1	0.28
(c) Other*	T			2	0.56	2	0.56
	R			2	0.56	2	0.56
	U						
B. Born outside India**	T	3	0.83			3	0.83
I. Bangladesh		2	0.56			2	0.56
II. Nepal		1	0.28			1	0.28

* include 2 vendors, one each from the states of Maharashtra and Uttar Pradesh.

**All belong to rural areas

Table 9 also gives the rural-urban origin of street food vendors. Majority (96.94%) of vendors have rural affiliation. Many of these vendors who were born in the rural areas have migrated to the city in search of livelihood.

Some of them have permanently migrated, having only limited connection to their rural roots, while others visit their natal home every year.

A look at the duration of stay of food vendors in Guwahati (Fig. 7) show that 72.22 per cent have lived in the city for over two years and 52.31 per cent of them even completed ten years of stay. 8.6 per cent of vendors currently operating in the city are seasonal migrants who have been coming to Guwahati regularly for the past 8 to 10 years. They live in rural areas of Assam and West Bengal and come for a few months. Only 19 per cent are recent migrants who are yet to complete two years of stay in Guwahati.

The forces and factors and necessary conditions under which vendors migrate and adjust in the new setting have been analyzed. In the context of the street food vendors of Guwahati, some of the important factors of migration may broadly be attributed to push factors such as rural poverty arising out of pressure of population on land, fragmentation of agricultural land and pull factors such as better job prospects in the cities with higher wages, etc. Other causes of migration are maladjustment in the joint family, excommunication from the village and petty crimes.

The migrants rarely move out of their original place without some information of the new setting. It is often seen that street food vendors derive information primarily from fellow villagers, who may or may not be kins, and who have already migrated to Guwahati. These people when they visit their natal village carry information for the other prospective migrants. Studies have shown (Rao 1974:7-13; 1986:31) that social network including kinship, caste and village language is the most effective medium by which information reaches the would-be-migrants. This is generally true in the case of street food vendors of Guwahati.

Satya Narayan Shah, aged 44 years, migrated to Assam about 27 years ago. He left his natal home in the Champaran district of Bihar when he was 17 years of age. He ran away from home after a quarrel with his father. He took a train to Patna, the capital of Bihar and stayed aimlessly for a few days till he met Babu Ram from the same village who worked as a rickshaw puller in Guwahati. With Babu Ram's aid he came to Assam. Here, Babu Ram arranged for a rickshaw on hire basis and for a few days he started pulling rickshaw in the streets of the city. Due to lack of experience and poor health he could not continue rickshaw pulling. Undecided about what to do next, he joined a nearby hotel in Birubari area of the city as a dish washer. More work and less money drove him away from this job. He stayed without work for a few days and during this period he (used to watch the neighbourhood food vendors) found out about a sweetmeat making unit in the Kalapahar area of the city. There are numerous vendors who buy sweetmeats like sohnpapri, peda, and sandesh and then sell it in different parts of the city. Satya Narayan also borrowed two saucepans from one such vendor (who went to his natal home) and started selling sweetmeats in Birubari and Bhangagarh areas.

Suresh Tiwari (32), who has been selling tea, bun, cake, biscuit and pakoras for the past eight years, is like any other roadside vendor in the city. He dropped out of school in class II, after the death of his father. Lack of adequate land for cultivation and of support from his elder brothers forced him to migrate from his village, in the border between Bihar and Uttar Pradesh. He came to Calcutta on the advice of a person from the same village who also worked there. Promised of some work, Suresh arrived in Calcutta, but this person was not there. So, Suresh stayed on in Calcutta looking for work. Lack of education and experience of any kind made matters worse for him till he found a part-time job in a tea stall. He worked as a helper in this stall for about two years when he decided to come to Guwahati to join his maternal uncle in the tea stall business.

It has been observed that migrants belonging to a particular region, language, religion and caste have a tendency to live together, at least in the initial stage. Vendors mostly migrate alone, leaving behind their wife and children in their village. The new vendors are accommodated by the earlier migrants who help them in finding jobs and in getting acquainted with the urban way of life.

Shibu Ram (41) is the second son of a cultivator in Motihari district of Bihar. His father left very little agricultural land (5 hectares) for him and his two brothers which they used to cultivate jointly. Even after the marriage of his elder brother, this practice continued. Problem arose only after Shibu's marriage when both the sister-in-laws frequently quarrelled over petty matters. The joint family had to separate and the property was divided equally among the three brothers. While the elder lived in the ancestral home with his mother and unmarried brother, Shibu and his wife separated and built a new but close to the old one. Shibu found it difficult to manage with the meagre income from the small plot of land. He worked as a part-time labour in the neighbouring village during harvesting.

When things became difficult, Shibu decided to come to the city of Patna to look for jobs. It was then that his distant relative, *chacha* (uncle), who worked as a rickshaw puller in Guwahati, apprised him of several opportunities there. At first, he was hesitant because Guwahati was far from his natal village but *chacha*'s assurance of finding a job and accommodation made him decide immediately.

The first generation migrants to towns and cities in India, as a rule, keep their rural roots alive. This is particularly so when parts of the family-parents, siblings, wife and children remain behind in the home community and when there is some land to cultivate at the disposal of the family. The rural migrant in such a case is very much a seasonal urban dweller and go home only periodically, especially to take part in agricultural work at peak times of planting and harvesting. This is found to be true of the sellers of street food in Guwahati. Though a substantial proportion of them (53%) have landed interest back home where their family kins live, in most cases income from agriculture is not enough to sustain the family[7].

There are, however, a large number of vendors who have no land. They have migrated to the city in search of some means of livelihood. Street food vending, as Bapat has observed (Sharma 1996), is an "easy-to-enter, non-capital intensive industry" as compared to the formal sector and other options available in the city. It should be mentioned that street food vending is not the immediate occupation of such vendors after coming to the city. On an average, a vendor changes his occupation at least two times before taking to food vending and in most cases, they have had past experience of working in restaurants or tea stalls.

Krishna Kalita (21) is the son of an Assamese cultivator from Bordewa in Nowgong district of Assam. He is the eldest son in a family consisting of six members. His father, who was the only earning member (from a small family farm), found it difficult to maintain the family. So, Krishna had to find work. Without an education to aid him, he found a job as a hotel waiter in Nowgong - headquarter of the district. While working there he befriended a bus conductor who informed him about job prospects in Guwahati.

After coming to Guwahati, he tried hard to find a job. After 10 days he was hired as a dishwasher-cum-kitchen hand in one of the smaller restaurants in the city. His salary was meagre but food and accommodation were free. He stayed there for about four years after which he decided to open his own food stall. Having considerable knowledge in the tea-stall business, he hired a push cart and started vending tea, bun, biscuit, *khurma, paratha, ghugni* and *pakora* (only in winter) near the city bus stop of the Guwahati Medical College Hospital at Bhangagarh.

Occupational pattern

Street food vending is a permanent occupation for many vendors. There are others who practise this activity as a secondary and as a part-time occupation. Table 10 gives the distribution of vendors according to occupation.

Table 10 shows that as many as 293 (81.4%) out of 360 vendors take up this activity as their main source of livelihood. Only 67 (18.6%) vendors sell different types of food as a supplementary source of income over and

Table 5.10: Distribution of Street Food Vendors According to Occupation

Occupation	*Type of Vendors*					
	Stationary		*Mobile*		*Total*	
	No.	*%*	*No.*	*%*	*No.*	*%*
Primary	89	24.72	204	56.67	293	81.4
Secondary	11	3.06	56	15.55	67	18.60
Total	100	27.77	260	72.66	360	100

above their main occupation. The primary occupation of this group of vendors include agriculture, masonry, carpentry, wage labour, fishing, rickshaw pulling, etc. As entry into the informal sector and also of food vending is relatively easy requiring limited skill and minimum of investment, it can be undertaken as a casual activity whenever the need arises.

PrakashBabu (42) belongs to the Mallah (boat man) caste of Bihar. He is a fisherman by occupation. Prakash along with eight other fellow fishermen have been catching fish in the Brahmaputra River in Guwahati for the past 10 years. But due to a fish epidemic some years ago, they were prohibited from fishing in the river as well as in the ponds. Since Prakash could not sell fish, it was becoming increasingly difficult to meet his day-to-day expenses. He decided to do some stray jobs like earth cutting, wage labourer etc. till he could resume his regular fishing. As his knowledge and skill was limited to fishing only, he could not adjust to other jobs easily. Incidentally in the place where Prakash used to live (in Manipuri Basti), there are a number of small manufacturers of finger chips, chocolates, sohnpapri, hawamithai, pankhamithai, etc. There are vendors who buy these and sell them in different parts of the city. Prakash decided to try his hand at it and started by selling sohnpapri, hawa and pankhamithai. He obtained a week's credit and also borrowed the box necessary to carry these items. With this he made a beginning in street food vending.

Sometimes a person while having a regular job take to street food vending as a part-time activity. This is so because the opportunity of making an additional income exists.

Sankha Das (46) is a night watchman in a small factory near the Assam Bengal Carrier (ABC) in the Guwahati-Shillong (G.S.) Road. He lives near the factory along with his wife and four children. His salary as a night watchman is not sufficient to feed, clothe and educate his children. So, he decided to open a small tea stall primarily to provide tea and along with it roti and sabji for the factory workers. Though the factory workers were not many in number, yet it provided him with ready customers. His wife helped him by preparing the sabji and at times by making the roti. Gradually other customers like rickshaw and *thela* pullers became his permanent customers and Sankha's wife prepares meals for them along with her family's. Sankha's children (only the elder two), when they do not go to school, help their parents in vending by running errands like carrying tea glasses to the factory, etc.

Sankha is earning more than his salary in the factory yet he does not want to leave the job. In future he would like to expand his stall and someday hope to open his own restaurant.

A large majority of street food vendors live in the city except 8.6 per cent of them who live in the rural areas and come to the city only for a few months. They are the Bengali seasonal migrants who come every year during the lean agricultural season (May-October) to sell sweetmeats and groundnuts. The sweetmeat seller come from West Bengal, while the groundnut sellers hail from parts of Nowgong district of Assam.

Dilip Kumar Saha (35) is the owner of a shop selling flower seedlings and tree saplings in the Barddhaman district of West Bengal. He has been visiting Guwahati regularly for the past 10 years. He along-with 24 other people belonging to Moira and Suri (maker of country liquor) castes who come for a period of five months from Jeth (May-June) to Ahin (September-October). They come from different villages in the Barddhaman district of West Bengal.

Dilip brings with him sufficient quantities of mihidana and prepares the sugar syrup in Guwahati to make the final sweetmeat. He along with his fellow peddlers have rented a four roomed house in Kalapahar, at a monthly rent of Rs. 1,500. Dilip and his fellow vendors make mihidana which they vend in different areas of the city[8]. Dilip sells in Uzanbazar, Kharghuli, Chenikuthi and Guwahati Club from about mid-morning till evening or till the stock lasts.

For Dilip and his friends, this is a secondary activity. All of them possesses agricultural land of varying proportions. To supplement income and to keep their traditional caste occupation alive they have taken to sweet making and selling. Temporary and seasonal migration of sweetmeat sellers have also been observed by Sinha (1986:300). These sweetmeat sellers go from 24 Paragana district of West Bengal to Ranchi in Bihar every year to sell sitabhog and mihidana.

Occupational mobility

Information about occupational mobility was collected from street food vendors about their family occupations. Data collected regarding three generations viz., ego's, parental and grand parental show that cultivation predominated in grand parental and parental generations. Besides cultivation, occupations like sweetmeat making, goldsmith, blacksmith, potters, oil pressers, makers of country liquor, chanachur selling, rickshaw pulling, boatmen and fishing was also found in the grand parental generation which gradually declined in the parental generation and almost absent in the ego's generation. Only five occupations - fishing, sweetmeat making and tea shop keeping (including pakora selling), rickshaw pulling, agriculture and chanachur selling show continuity into the ego's generation. In the study sample, chanachur, pakora and sweetmeat making and selling show continuity as street food vending occupation in the three generations. This group of vendors constitutes 9.1 per cent. It includes 25 Bengali sweetmeat makers and tea stall owners, 6 Bihari chanachur sellers, 1 Bihari pakora seller and 1 Assamese vendor whose father owned a tea stall in his natal village. The rest of the street food vendors do not show any indication of food vending as a family tradition.

Madhav Mahato (63) is one of the oldest chanachur vendor in Guwahati. As a small boy he migrated to Guwahati along with his father and three brothers from Simanjila in Bihar because income from the tiny plot of land was not enough. They came just before the Second World War. In those days his father, Juguna used to sell chanachur from a box which he carried on one shoulder with the help of a strap. While his brothers diversified into other occupations, Madhav took up his father's occupation. He bought a box with conical bamboo stand and with this he vended chanachur by roaming the streets of Guwahati. Now-a-days he sells from a covered pushcart (with a valid license for slow moving vehicle) and has two regular spots. In the morning, he sells in front of Handique Girl's College from about 11 a.m. till 3 p.m. and later in the evening from 5 p.m. till about 8 p.m. he vends in Panbazar.

Madhav is married with a son and daughter both of whom are married. His son stays with him. Though he owns a pan shop, he is usually busy helping his father in the preparation and sale of chanachur.

TYPES OF VENDORS

The street food vendors in Guwahati can be categorized by the types of food sold : relish, snacks, light meals, meals, sweetmeat, fruits, etc.[9]; and nature of vending : into stationary and mobile vendors. The stationary vendors are those who sell from a fixed location throughout the day. These vendors usually sell from a shop10, stall11, or carts12. In Guwahati, these carts are not permitted to be mobile by the Guwahati Municipal Corporation Authorities except those having a license for slow moving vehicle. Stationary vendors sell items of food like tea, bun, biscuit, cake, cream roll, nimki, malpua, jilebi, chop, pakora, omlette, boiled eggs, groundnut, popcorns, makkai, roll, pulao, chowmein, roti-sabji and meals (vegetarian and non- vegetarian).

The mobile vendors are those that do not sell at one location only but move about from place to place in search of customers. There are broadly two kinds of mobile vendors, the first moves about in a definite route by making fixed rounds. The sellers of chanachur (those selling from big push carts and boxes), phuska (those selling from small push carts),jhalmuri, ice cream, etc. follow a definite route every day. They are seen in front of the school in the morning before school starts, then in the afternoon during recess and after school hours. In between, they gravitate to the nearby cinema hall or proceed to the market place or street corners.

The second type of the vendors are more mobile than the first. Such vendors have an area earmarked and within that specified area carries on vending activities. A vendor is not supposed to trespass into each other's territory, which are jealously guarded. Mobile vendors sell items like chanachur, jhalmuri, bhelpuri, phuska, hawamithai, pankhamithai, dosa, groundnuts, popcorns, sohnpapri, rasogolla, mihidana, sitabhog, sandesh, different varieties of laddus, slices of fruits like coconut, cucumber, pineapple, papaya, watermelon, etc. To sell all these types of food, mobile vendors take the help of small carts, boxes, wooden tray, dish, bamboo baskets etc.

Though the study sample consists of 100 stationary and 260 mobile vendors, it is seen that in reality, a few vendors are really mobile in the sense that they are constantly on the move throughout the day. Even those vendors who sell from wheeled carts sell from one or two definite places every day. While some vendors had two daily spots, others moved over to the zoological garden or children's park on Sundays. Even vendors who carry baskets or boxes and are highly mobile tend to come to a particular location in the evening. Only a few sellers of sweetmeat, laddu and fruit slices are really mobile. Thus, it is apparent that truly mobile vendors are rare.

Location of vendors

The choice of location by a vendor is very important. They usually cluster only where there are customers, near schools, hospitals, bus stops, courts, railway and bus station, market places, etc. The location of vendors in Guwahati city and the importance of each location is highlighted in Table 5.11.

Table 11 shows the main vending areas of Guwahati city. These areas encompass commercial, residential and mixed commercial and office areas.

Table 5.11: The Main Vending Areas of Street Food Vendors in Guwahati

Areas	*Descriptions*
Fancy bazar	Main commercial area, deals in textiles, hardware, vegetables, etc.
Athgaon	Commercial area, truck stand
Paltan bazar	Commercial and transport centre, railway and bus station
Bhangagarh	Mixed commercial and office area, Guwahati Medical College and Hospital
Dispur (Ganeshguri)	Commercial, residential and office areas Temporary Capital complex
Khanapara	Administrative and educational centre. Assam Agricultural University
Uzan bazar	Residential and commercial areas
Chandmari	Residential and commercial areas
Noonmati and Narengi	Commercial and mixed residential areas. New Guwahati Railway station, Oil refinery, Military Cantonment, Industrial estate, etc.
Zoo-Narengi	Commercial and residential area, State Zoological Garden
Maligaon (Pandu)	Transport, commercial and residential areas, Headquarter of N.F. Railways, Adabari (previously at Bhutnath) Bus stand
Jalukbari	Educational and residential areas, Gauhati University, Assam Engineering College, etc.
National Highway No. 37 by-pass (Jalukbari to Khanapara)	Area of transport and commercial activity

Besides the areas already mentioned in the table, there are some main roads along which vendors are found in greater intensity (Fig. 6). Some of these are also the routes of city bus, which are used by a large number of commuters every day. Over and above the city bus stops, a large concentration of vendors (both stationary and mobile) is found near the truck stands at Athgaon, Fancy bazar and New Guwahati railway station; National Highway No. 37 by - pass, Capital complex at Dispur, Medical College Hospital at Bhangagarh, near the Deputy Commissioner's court, cinema halls, motor garages, parks, fair grounds, market places, etc.

SOCIO-CULTURAL LIFE AND BEHAVIOUR PATTERNS OF STREET FOOD VENDORS

The socio-cultural life and behaviour patterns of street food vendors are to a considerable extent determined by various forces and factors related to street food vending. Social needs are fulfilled not only within one's familial or neighborhood close-knit group, but involve a series of independent relationships.

Street food vending is hard work permitting very little leisure time for the vendors. They work from early morning till late at night, through all days of the week. Whatever little time they get, they utilize for personal work like washing clothes and cleaning the house, etc. However, there are a few stationary vendors, who operate near offices, educational institutions, financial establishments, major commercial and business areas, etc. who take the Sundays off. For many others like the mobile vendors, Sundays and other holidays are busy times. They sell near cinema halls, parks, zoo, etc. From whatever free time they can manage, the vendors spend by relaxing, usually with the family or by visiting relatives, temples and occasionally by going to the cinema. Besides these, vendors spend time by watching television (in the neighbourhood), listening to the radio, gossiping, drinking and gambling.

Sudhakar Babu (50) is a Bihari seller of muri and cira laddu in Guwahati. He lives along with five other street food vendors in a two-roomed house in Chaatribari (near A.T. Road). His family lives in Darbhanga district of Bihar. Sudhakar sells on all days of the week from about 10 in the morning till 6 in the evening. Every Saturday from about 7.30 p.m., after all his room-mates return, Sudhakar and his friends go to a shack where country liquor is sold. There they drink and play cards till about 11 o'clock at night. After having their night meal in a nearby street stall they return home.

Kon Chandra Kalita (39) is an inhabitant of Noonmati hillside (since 1987). He is married and lives along with his wife and children in Noonmati. But mounting expenditure of keeping a family in the city and problems of ancestral property in his natal village (Solmara in Nalbari district) made him shift his family, in 1991, back to his village.

He sells roti-sabji, ghugni, pulao and meals (only occasionally) near the Dispur Capital complex. On Sundays and other holidays when the offices are closed, he visits his family in the village. Sometimes, when the offices remain closed for three to four days together, he stays in the village for a few more days during which period his shop remains closed. Sometimes he engages his friend to run the shop.

The street food vendors operating in Guwahati come from a diverse regional, social and cultural background, they share certain common features by which they are distinguishable from other groups of people. Street food vending as a distinct economic activity which shapes the attitude and cultural outlook of the vendors. The mode and size of income provide a particular status to the vendor and his family. Thus economic activity (occupation), status and cultural outlook are correlated.

Subjective features like attitudes, behaviour patterns, outlook towards life vary among the vendors. It is closely linked to income. As income increases, the "life chances" or social opportunities also become better. Vendors who have a life of hardship and drudgery, bogged with problems, have a fatalistic attitude towards life and generally depressed. This is also true for vendors who have had to face frequent harassment and dislocation in trading. This feeling of uncertainty generally restricts a vendor from expanding in the trade. Vendors who have been successful are optimistic and desire to innovate.

Street food vendors in spite of their uncertain conditions are not indifferent to religious practices and beliefs. They are God-fearing people. Most vendors keep pictures and idols of Lord Ganesh and Lakshmi (Hindu deities associated with prosperity) in their carts and boxes. Every morning floral oblations to God are made and incense sticks are lit. After lighting the stove to start cooking, the vendor prays by offering a little bit of the food (to be cooked) into the fire place.

Vendors are by and large superstitious and fear the evil eye. Many of them take recourse to evading the evil eye. Vendors are seen suspending a lemon and few chilies from the roof of the cart.

It has been observed that vendors have a fascination for colouring their carts brightly and attractively. Also, they show a liking towards naming their carts. Names are often given after Hindu Gods and Goddesses like Krishna, Shiva, Durga, Kali and Santoshi. Sometimes carts are named after family members of the vendors like mother, wife and children. At times names are also related to popular food like "Popular Chaat House" or "Bombay Bhelpuri", etc.

So far in this chapter, an outline of street food vendors has been made. It identifies the people who make and sell street food in Guwahati. Also, their socio-demographic features have been discussed. It is evident that the food vendors operating in Guwahati are largely non-Assamese people who have migrated to Assam. They have very little education and skill for other jobs and take up this activity which can be learnt easily.

The following chapter, Chapter Six gives details of the street food trade in Guwahati.

Notes

1. As Cantlie notes, "As the Assamese villager preferred the cultivation of his own fields to wage labour on a tea garden, it became necessary to import labourers mainly from Bihar and Orissa... Today migrants still come to work on roads and construction industries...that the Assamese do not do...*(Also)* in the absence of an indigenous entrepreneurial class Marwaris and Punjabis have settled in the state..." (1984: x-xi). Words in italics are mine.
2. It is the highest among the Sudra varna caste of Assam.
3. This caste is divided into two types, Halowa (ploughing) and Jalowa (fishing). The Halowas are considered to be superior.
4. The Koch is an agricultural caste. This caste is supposed to have been originally formed as a result of Sanskritization of the various tribal groups to Hinduism.
5. For details of Assamese caste see Cantlie 1984:7-23, 182, 223-253, 305-312; Hutton 1951:213; McSwiney 1912.
6. It is the ninth month of the Islamic calendar during which period Muslim people are required to fast during the day.
7. The average size of a street food vendor's family is 6.75.
8. While some people buy from them off the street, they mainly rely on door-to-door selling in the city neighbourhood.
9. These categories have already been discussed in Chapter Four.
10. A shop is a room having fewer than four permanent walls (Tinker 1987:52).
11. A stall for the purpose of selling street food may be a box or a table on which goods are arranged for sale.
12. A street food vendors' cart is a two-wheeled (small) or a four-wheeled (big) vehicle, motorized or not, which may be moved about or kept stationary.

Chapter - 6

The Street Food Trade

The street food trade in Guwahati is primarily an activity carried out by the rural migrants who come to the city in order to eke out an income for survival. Although Assam does not have a tradition of street food, it has proliferated like the other informal sector activities. Earlier, cooking and serving of food were the tasks traditionally carried out by the womenfolk of the household, while men worked outside the house to earn their livelihood in non-domestic activities. The processes associated with cooking of food were generally confined to the domestic hearth. As soon as this activity began to have an economic relevance, as a source of income, men took it upon themselves to earn their livelihood through this pursuit. The kitchen which was earlier confined to the house became a part of the street and along with it the hearth "encounters a socio-cultural heterogeneity" (Khare 1976:12). It is increased further with changes in education, occupation, migration and the emergence of a secular society and its norms at large (*ibid.*).

THE ENTERPRISE

Street food vending is a part and parcel of city life in Guwahati. The enterprises1 are mostly run as one-man unit. They account for 82 per cent of the total vending outlets in the city. The rest includes six enterprises run by married couples, twenty five joint ventures between brothers and one three member enterprise between two brothers and a friend. There are some vendors who engage or employ additional labour from various sources. Table 1 shows the kind of additional labour used in the trade.

Table 1 indicates that family sources including the wife, unmarried children and brothers help in a majority of cases. The vendors whose families do not reside in Guwahati take the help of unmarried brothers, friends, etc. Hired help is engaged by vendors in addition to family help. These workers

Table 6.1 : Types of Additional Workers Used in Street Food Trade

Type of worker	*M*		*F*	*T*
Family workers	%	40 18.01 (10)*	123 55.40 (6)	163 73.42 (16)
Hired worker	%	49 22.07 (18)	1 0.45	50 22.52 (18)
Others**	%	9 4.05 98	124	9 4.05 222
Total	%	44.14	55.85	100

* Figures in parentheses indicate minor workers.

**This category includes friends or casual workers who do not get wages.

may be employed temporarily on a daily wage basis or on a permanent one with monthly salary. These hired workers are mostly men (49) and include a fair number of boys (18).

Babul Shah (42) is a Bihari immigrant from Sarsopahi area of Madhubani district of Bihar. He has been selling puri, ghugni, chop and bread pakora from a roadside cart near the Dispur capital complex for the past ten years. Since last four years, he has been selling regularly on festive occasions like Rongali Bihu and Durga Puja. During these festivals, he pushes his cart (he has a license for slow moving vehicle, hence by law permitted to be mobile) to a convenient location near the festival site. Besides vending in the usual food items, Babul prepares pakora, khurma and coconut laddu.

Last year (1991) he hired two boys (aged 19 and 12 years) during Durga Puja to help him in serving, washing utensils and carrying water. Babul said that he could engage the boys because sale was three times more during these days. He paid the older boy ₹ 40.00 and the younger one ₹ 20.00 per day for four days.

There are many vendors who employ additional labour during festivals (Bihu and Puja), fairs (Guwahati Book Fair) and exhibitions (Craft Bazar, Handloom exhibitions) etc. (Plate 28). After they are over, such extra labourers are removed. But home help remains by and large a constant source of labour for the vendors. The division of labour within the household, with regard to buying, processing and cooking the food to be sold is largely a family affair.

Rathin (29) is a seller of roti, ghugni, dal and tarkari/sabji near the Dispur capital complex. He lives along with his wife, Runu in Sarumataria about 1 km. from the place of sale. They have been married for two years and together prepare the food to be sold. Rathin does the shopping for all the raw materials necessary in the process of preparing the food like flour, chick peas, potatoes, dal, seasonal vegetables, spices, etc. Once a week he buys these ingredients. Every night it is Runu's duty to soak the chick peas. In the early morning, she prepares the ghugni and the dal while Rathin cuts and washes the vegetables for the tarkari. He then arranges the food to be taken to the place of sale. At about 8 a.m., after eating a light meal, he transports these items on a rickshaw and leaves for his pushcart (stationary).

Here, the first thing he does is to clean the place. Then he brings water from the nearby tap and stores it in tin drums to be used the entire day. Thereafter he starts kneading the dough for the roti and starts cooking the vegetables to be ready by 9 a.m. when the customers start coming. They come for various works in the secretariat and other offices in the capital complex.

Rathin has no help in the cart. He serves and washes the plates himself. Sometimes in the afternoon, Runu joins him and help by washing the utensils and also by serving. But with regard to cooking in the place of sale, Rathin does it entirely.

Home help is used in processing and preparing street food. Members of the vendor's family, particularly the wife, help at home by cleaning and cooking the food to be sold. Usually, a vendor's wife does not go to the vending spot except when the need for assistance arises.

Gauranga Paul (48) is a Bengali seller hailing from the state of West Bengal. He is married and lives in a rented room in Maligaon area of the city. He is engaged in selling puri, ghugni and chaat in Maligaon where the head quarter of N.F. Railway is situated. In addition, he sells in the book fair held in the Judge's field every year. For the past three years he has been selling puri, ghugni, chaat in the fair site. On the night before the opening day, he places his cart in a convenient location near the entrance of the fair. His cart is brightly painted and gaily decorated with flower garlands. The cart is provided with a roof and kept open on all sides. On one side of the cart are the puffed puris neatly stacked one over the other which is prepared on the spot with the help of kerosene pressure stoves. The chaat is decorated with a salad and placed on a tray over a lighted stove. Besides these, the cart also contains space for a saucepan (containing ghugni) and another stove which is used for making tea.

This year, as the visitors to the fair increased, Paul found it difficult to cope even with two additional helpers (aged 12 and 14 years) who were mostly used for washing the utensils and carrying water from the tap at a distance of about 50 ft. On the fourth day of the ten day fair he asked his wife Ruma to join him. Normally, she does not visit the establishment but because of increased demand she came and helped her husband by preparing tea and collecting money. At home, she helps her husband by cutting, cleaning, soaking and cooking the different ingredients necessary for preparing next day's food.

Hari Prasad Mondal, aged 45 years, is a cultivator from Bebejia near Nowgong in Assam. He grows mainly a crop of jute and some groundnuts. He supplements his income by resorting to groundnut selling in Guwahati during the agriculturally lean season. Hari Prasad said that his wife, Kunjabala, in addition to her domestic chores helps him by cleaning and drying the groundnuts and also by packing the sacks to be transported to Guwahati.

Level of investment

Street food vendors like other workers in the informal sector do not generally keep written accounts of investment and income. However, in-depth interviews of the individual vendors have revealed that levels of investment varied from vendor to vendor. It depends upon several factors like the type of food sold, nature of establishment and economic condition of the vendor.

Bani Saha (36) is a Bengali widow with two children. She hails from a village in Dhubri district of Assam about 290 kms. west of Guwahati. She came to Guwahati ten years ago after her marriage to Raju Saha, a steel trunk maker. Seven years after their marriage, Raju died leaving Bani with very little money and two small children. Burdened with past debts and no work, she was desperate to find some means of sustenance. After a few futile attempts she decided to start a small tea stall just outside her house. She lives in Panbazar-Ranibari area in a small two-roomed rented house. It is a commercial area comprising of several pharmaceutical firms as well as shops dealing in books, stationeries, watches, etc. From a few street food vendors in the area, she found out how with the minimum of investment she could start a business of her own. She got a loan of ₹ 250.00 from her landlord (who was also kind enough to waive a portion of her house rent till she could establish herself) with which she bought tea leaves (1 kg.), milk powder (1 kg.), sugar (1 kg.), kerosene (5 litres) and a stove total expenditure of which was ₹ 200.00. She also bought bun (2 doz.), biscuit (3 doz.) and cake (1 doz.) on credit2. Thus, with a very nominal expense of approximately ₹ 200.00, Bani started vending in a very humble manner.

Sailen Das (27) hails from Rangia (52 kms. north of Guwahati) in Kamrup district. He used to sell flowers in Guwahati. Now he sells chowmein, pulao, ghugni/choley-bhatura and tea from a pushcart located near the Latasil playground.

Initially he started by selling from a small table (only for a month), but later on he bought a new cart for ₹ 1200.00. It is glass covered on three sides. He also bought two kerosene pressure stoves, stainless steel plates and glasses, cast iron cooking receptacles and two wooden benches. He also provided a plastic sheet over the sitting area (very close to the wall of the Latasil play ground) for shade and protection from rain. All these had cost him (in 1991) about ₹ 3000.00. In addition, buying of raw materials involves added expenditure of approximately ₹ 300.00 daily. All these expenses were possible partly from his personal savings and partly from a loan of ₹ 1,500.00 from two flower sellers.

Initial Capital

Capital is an essential requirement to start any business. The street food vendors were asked where the initial capital came from to invest in the business. The table below gives the sources of initial capital used by street food vendors in Guwahati.

Table 2 shows that personal savings is the highest source of initial capital. Close relatives contribute about 20.28 per cent followed by friends who offered interest-free loans to 15.56 per cent of enterprises. Money lenders form another important source (8.06%) of starting capital. Loans

Table 6.2 : Sources of Initial Capital of The Vendors

Sources	*Vendors*	
	No	*%*
Personal savings	201	55.83
Family Sources	73	20.28
Money lender	29	8.06
Friends	56	15.56
Bank	1	0.28
Total	360	100.00

from banks are not popular. Except for one, who received bank loan, there are two Assamese and one Bihari vendors who sought bank loans to buy pushcarts and to start business. But because of complicated paper work and procedures of banks, they had to approach Bihari money lenders who offered the money instantly, but at a very high rate of interest.

Daily credit on a particular day was also common (48.32%). However, many vendors felt that their costs would be reduced if they could buy in greater quantities, but capital remains a major problem for many vendors.

Raju Das (29), son of an Assamese daily wage labourer, sells paratha, ghugni, pulao and chowmein near a cinema hall in Maligaon. He is married with a new born baby and lives in a rented room in Maligaon railway colony. He hired a pushcart (but vends from a fixed location) from a Bihari person at a monthly rent of ₹ 400.00.

He gets good clientele consisting of cinema-goers and other casual marketers. On an average, in a day, he manages to make a profit of approximately ₹ 100. But there are several expenses like house rent (₹ 150 p.m.), hiring charges of the cart (₹ 400 p.m.), encroachment fee of ₹ 5 to be paid to the municipality every day and food and other expenditures. This makes bulk buying of the raw materials (to prepare food) very difficult.

In street food trading, business and personal finance are inseparable because of the close connection between home and work. Thus, whenever emergency arises like illness of the vendor, his family members or to meet incidental expenses or social commitments, there is a likelihood of using business money for personal needs. This is because alternative source of money at low interest hardly exists as opposed to money for business. This tendency of small entrepreneurs to mix personal and business money is seen as a limiting factor for further investment and expansion by the development economists.

Ram Khelam Shah (59) is a seller of tea, bun, biscuit and chaat from a roadside stall consisting of a wooden bed. His stall is located near the Kamakhya funeral ground in Bhutnath. He lives along with his wife (50) just behind the stall in a one roomed house. Shah, despite his small investment (less than ₹ 500) makes good business. His stall caters to all the nearby shops like cycle repair shop, motor garage, rickshaw and thela pullers, woodcutters and people coming to the funeral ground. Despite all these, he has not been able to increase his inventory of food. Money is the biggest problem for him. His wife who is ailing needs medical attention from time to time. So whatever little profit he gets from the vending outlet goes for medical expenses and little is left for reinvestment.

Bipin Deka, aged 40 years, hails from Nalbari district of Assam. He is married and has three children. They all live in a rented house in Beltola area. Bipin used to sell tea, bun, cake, biscuit, etc. in a stall near the Wireless bus stop in the same area. Two months back his father died. Being the only son, it was customary to fulfil all the ritual and social obligations associated with the mortuary ceremony which is very expensive. On completion of the death rituals, he along with his family returned to Guwahati to find that his temporary shed was demolished by the Guwahati Municipal Authorities. After they dismantled his shop, he could not rebuild it for about a month. By that time, whatever little savings he had was exhausted. He looked around for a small loan to build a shed. After a long search, his brother-in-law gave him a loan of ₹ 300 only. Since this money was not sufficient, a friend of his advised him to meet a person who would be helpful. Bipin met the person who is the owner of several rickshaws and pushcarts and received ₹ 1,000.00 with an interest of 5 per cent per month. He built the stall in the same location and started work. As business picked up and old customers started coming, he was able to regain his earlier position.

Income and its Uses

After estimating daily cost and observing sale, it is possible to divide the enterprises into three income groups : low income group (LIG) with a daily income of less than ₹ 40.00, middle income group (MIG) between ₹ 40.00 to ₹ 80.00 per day and high income group (HIG) having a daily income of above ₹ 80.00. Using this criterion, the street food enterprises of Guwahati have been divided accordingly as shown in Fig. 8.

Of the total number of enterprises, 173 (52.90%) belong to the lower income group, followed by 124 (37.92%) in the middle and 30 (9.2%) in the high income group respectively (Table: 6.3). The average daily income is ₹ 50.00. This income is more than that of a daily wage labourer. However, income depends upon several factors, some of which are location, type of food, seasonality, etc.

(i) Location : The location of street food sellers is important. Vendors tend to gravitate wherever the customers are concentrated. Prime locations are courts, hospitals, government offices and establishments, cinema halls, market places, main roads, etc.

(ii) Food type : In addition to location, food type sold is also an important factor contributing to income of street food vendors. A vendor must assess the demand for a particular food in a locality. For instance, Sita Ram is a chana vendor in Guwahati. He prefers to sell near schools, park, cinema halls and in market places because people who go to these places have very little time and chana can be eaten while standing with minimum of fuss. Moreover, this relish by its very sight can cause demand. By observing the customers of this vendor in a day (total: 118 customers), it was found that chana is eaten primarily by the Bihari (78), Marwari (28), Assamese (8), Punjabi (3) and Bengali (1) communities. Secondly, more than half the customers are children (53%). The approximate sale in a day is about ₹ 100.00 leaving a net income of ₹ 30.00. The minimum price of one helping is ₹ 0.50.

The case of two vendors cited below will show how the choice of food in a particular location helps to increase income.

Dipak (23) and Ramesh (36) hail from Belsor, a village about 70 kms west of Guwahati. Together they started by selling juice of

Table 6.3: Distribution of Street Food Vending Enterprises According to Income Group

Income Enterprises	*Group*	
	No.	*%*
Lower income group (Less than ₹40/-per day)	173	52.90
Middle income group (Between ₹40/- to 80/- per day)	124	37.92
Higher income group (More than ₹ 80/-)	9.20	30
TOTAL	327	100.00

tender coconut[3] in front of the Deputy Commissioner's court in the city. After a year they gave up because they were not earning enough probably due to the presence of a large number of sellers of tender coconut in the same location.

They decided to start a street side eatery on a pushcart near the same site. With the help of a loan of ₹ 1000.00 partly from a friend and Dipak's sister's husband, they bought two pairs of benches, some utensils and two kerosene pressure stoves. Ramesh had past experience of working in a canteen as a waiter and kitchen hand. He cooks meals consisting of rice, dal and vegetable curry; roti, omelette and prepares snacks like bread pakora, malpua, etc. Dipak prepares tea and serves food to the customers.

They make brisk business on weekdays from 8 a.m. till about 6 p.m. when they get numerous customers. These people are employees of nearby offices and people coming from outside Guwahati for different kinds of business in these offices.

A cup of tea and a minimum snack cost ₹ 3.00, while a simple meal costs between ₹ 5.00 to ₹ 10.00. Their daily sale from this eatery leaves them with an income of ₹ 100.00 to ₹ 150.00 per day.

(iii) Seasonality : In Guwahati, street food vending during the rainy season (summer) is erratic. Many snacks and relishes which are vended and eaten on the street by standing are largely affected. In winter, despite shorter days, vending is good and income made in this season is better than summer. Also, the food type varies along with the change in season.

Religion and festive occasions, including fairs attract a large number of vendors. Durga puja, Idd, Rongali Bihu and fairs associated with Shivratri, ambubashi and Chaat puja attract and raise demand for street food. Conversely, religion may also restrict the sale of street food. In the Islamic month of Ramadan, many Muslim people keep fast. Also, in the month-of Chaut (March - April), when many Marwari and Bihari people fast, sale of street food declines.

During the busy period of planting and harvesting, vendors who have agricultural land in their natal homes leave the city for a period to come back again. This also affects sale.

Expansion of Trade

Expansion of street food trade is an indication of its viability. While most (88%) of the vendors in Guwahati would have liked some credit to improve inventories, very few vendors seemed eager to expand. There are many difficulties as voiced by several vendors in the expansion of the trade. These are hiring additional employees, meeting a payroll, finding larger place in which to make or sell street food and the 'risk' of operating without a license. In addition, the vendors fear that municipal regulations might be stricter on the slightly larger enterprises.

It is often seen that vendors do not invest in permanent structures. This is primarily because of the existing municipal rules 349(1)a and b and 354(1)b of the Guwahati Municipal Corporation Act, 1969, which prohibit erection of any structure on the roadside. Moreover, such erection requires prior permission of the engineer of the ward and Commissioner of the corporation. In order to obtain permission, a vendor must provide bona fide land records regarding ownership of land, payment of taxes, site plan, etc.

Instead of expanding the existing trade, vendors by and large prefer to invest in other directions. Interviews of street food vendors in Guwahati have revealed that 55 per cent of vendors regularly send home money to their families who live in their natal villages. The profit derived from street food vending is thus utilized in other directions. One of the main uses is for the maintenance of the family. Then comes education of children.

There are however a few vendors (16) who have expanded their enterprises. Enterprises with sufficient income tend to expand either laterally or hierarchically (Tinker 1987a:68). Lateral expansion is based on an amoeba model - one of replication. In most cases, lateral expansion is treated like a new enterprise run by another family member.

Upendra Pathak (43) is a phuska seller in the busy Fancy bazar area of the city. He left his native village Manichowk in the Sitamarhi district of Bihar some 20 years ago. At first, he went to Calcutta looking for a job. While in Calcutta, he picked up the skill of preparing phuska. He sold for 13 years in Calcutta after which he had to leave the place because young boys used to come and demand money from him often and trouble him. One day while he was visiting his native village, he met a muri laddu seller (of the same village) and informed him about Assam and about the immense scope of street food vending in Guwahati. Along with this friend, Upendra came to Guwahati and started making and selling phuska in the Lakhtokia area. Later he shifted to a better location near Shani Mandir area of Fancy Bazar. After seeing the business prospects here, few years later, he brought his two brothers to Guwahati to join him and help him in this trade. None of them knew earlier how to prepare phuska or any other street food. But they learnt it from Upendra and operated as individual vendors by selling in separate locations. They all live together in a rented house in Athgaon and prepare the snack together.

Expansion of street food trade can also take place along a hierarchical model of a pyramid. This expansion involves a vertical upgradation of the trade, from a simple level to a higher level. It may be by increasing inventory of food and by occupying more area.

Naba Bora (35) hails from a village in Nowgong district of Assam. He was working in a pharmaceutical company in Guwahati for 3 years, after which he had to leave the company due to a misunderstanding with the employer. He did not go back to his village, instead he took to selling tea, bun, biscuit and cake from a box in a street corner in Panbazar. Later he shifted to a bigger place (present site) in Panbazar. He bought a pushcart and remodelled it. He also erected temporary covers for the convenience of customers. In this present site he sells tea, chowmein, choley bhatura and rolls which are prepared from a gas and two kerosene pressure stoves. He has managed to employ 3 persons who help him is cooking and serving.

He has a number of steady customers including office workers, college students and nearby shopkeepers. He admits that this trade is very profitable and one can expand but space and municipal regulations are the major problems. Some day he hopes to own a restaurant and buy a truck which would help him in expanding his business.

Vertical expansion of street food trade may also involve such expansion leading to a complete changeover from street food vending to ownership of restaurant. During the period of this study, the present investigator found only one vendor (a graduate) who moved from food vending to restaurant ownership.

WOMEN IN STREET FOOD TRADE

Street food vending in Guwahati is dominated by men and women vendors comprise only 3.9 per cent of the total sample. In a country like India, which is predominantly patriarchal, men act as the head of the intact family. While the divorced, widowed or single women are controlled and protected by the male relatives. But in the context of this study, it is seen that with the rise of women-headed households, women's economic prowess has increased.

Dhannada Das (29) is an unmarried Assamese woman hailing from a village 70 kms north west of Guwahati. She is the third child in a family consisting of a widowed mother, two elder brothers who are married and two younger sisters who are studying. Dhannada is a matriculate and could have got a job in a government office, but after several attempts she had to forego the idea. Instead, she wanted to do something on her own. She used to come every day by bus to Guwahati to sell hand woven gamocha and chaddar and return home in the evening. This proved to be strenuous and unprofitable. Meanwhile her mother was seriously ill and required constant attention. Her brothers refused to look after their mother. So, the responsibility was entirely upon Dhannada.

They had very little agricultural land which was divided among the two brothers. So, Dhannada decided to come to Guwahati and with the assistance of her uncle (distant kin who is also from the same village) who started a small vending stall adjoining the main bus stop near Judge's field. She sells tea, bun, biscuit, cake and tambul-pan. After a few months, when her business started picking up, she brought her mother to Guwahati but left her sisters with relatives in the village. Both of them lives in a small room in the Uzanbazar area of the city.

Besides fending for her mother and herself, Dhannada sends home money for the education and other expenses of her sisters.

Women's income is essential. It not only supplements the family's income but also gives her a sense of independence vital to herself respect and her position in the family. Though women vendors in Guwahati constitute a very small segment, the income derived by them are important for household economy. Out of fourteen vendors, six are the sole supporters of their family. They include five single women and one married woman whose husband is a drunkard with no income of his own. There are six vendors who work along with their husbands as a joint venture in this trade and two women vendors who work to supplement their husband's income.

In India, where patriarchy prevails, culture and religion demand that a woman be shy, retiring and generally confined to the precincts of the house. In Guwahati, the social restriction seemed less severe and more than half of the women vendors including the single, widowed or those married to men who did not work, have to work outside the house because of necessity (which is not conventional), in addition to their role as mother or wife.

Janki (32) is a Bihari woman married to a carpenter who used to work in a furniture shop in Kharghuli (near Uzanbazar market). He lost his job because he was a drunkard. Janki with two children (aged 4 and 2 years) had to work to subsist. She worked as a part-time domestic help (only one shift) in three households in the neighbourhood on a monthly payment of Rs. 100 each. Before the pay was due Janki's husband used to go to these households and take advance payment and spend it on drinking. Not knowing what to do, she started by opening a small sale counter of boiled eggs in the nearby market place. Every afternoon she took her two children, along and sold from about 3 p.m. till about 7 p.m. in the evening. Later, she expanded by selling tea, bun and biscuit. This business has contributed in a great way in meeting the growing expenses of her family.

Women's involvement in street food trade shows that women act as individual operators or as assistants to their husbands (in case of wife) in the place of sale and at home as unpaid home help. But when a woman vendor becomes successful, she is assisted by her husband or some other male relatives. However, the reverse is not true. When a man is successful, the first thing he does is to remove his wife from the business and in her place hired labourers are engaged.

It has been observed that female vendors spend more time in preparation of food and less time in vending. This is due to the fact that women have to tend to the house and look after children as well. Thus, it affects women's income.

Mina Roy (31) is a Bengali woman who sells roti-sabji and vegetarian meals near a construction site near Noonmati. She lives along with her husband and three children in the same location. Her husband is the gate keeper of the construction site and earns a salary of Rs. 500.00 per month. With this money Mina finds it difficult to make ends meet. So with her husband's approval (who also assists her) she began her enterprise. She serves afternoon meals on a contract basis to all the construction workers and other casual labourers engaged in the site. This gives her a net profit of Rs. 60-70 per day. She regrets that if she could sell for the entire day (she has to look after her new born child and do other household tasks), she would have made double the profit.

From the above discussion, it is apparent that this activity can be carried out by persons with little or no skill and with a nominal investment. The average income made from this activity is more than that of a daily wage earner in the city and equal to that of a semi-skilled worker. In spite of this activity permitting easy entry, requiring less skill and yielding a substantial return, it has not expanded. Financial constraint and municipal harassment are important factors which have restricted the street food vendors from expanding their trade.

Notes

1. An enterprise may be defined as an undertaking engaged in production and/or distribution of goods and/or distribution of goods and/ or services not for the sole purpose of own consumption. The workers in an enterprise may consist of members of the household or hired workers or both. The activities of the enterprise may be carried out at one or more than one distinct location. The activities of the enterprise may also be carried on only for a part of the year but on a fairly regular basis. It can be owned or operated by a single household or by several households jointly (on a partnership basis) or by an institutional body. (Source: Enterprise List, Census of India, 1991).
2. Credit is usually given for one day (daily credit), but in this case she was offered a week's credit on sympathy ground.
3. The tender coconut has a great demand during the hot season for its refreshing juice.

Chapter - 7

Street Food and Municipal Control

As the largest urban and commercial centre in N.E. India, Guwahati attracts thousands of visitors, traders, businessmen and workers from both within and outside the state. Being a centre of trade, commerce, administration and education, there has been a tremendous increase in population making it one of the most crowded cities in the eastern region. The population of Guwahati has grown from 2,52,305 in 1971 to 5,84,342 in 1991, with a density of 2,695 persons per sq. km. within an area of 216.78 sq. kms. As per provisional reports of Census India, population of Guwahati in 2011 is 957,352; of which male and female are 495,362 and 461,990 respectively. Although Guwahati city has population of 957,352; its urban / metropolitan population is 962,334. This explosive population increase has created pressure on urban infrastructure and services; and induced mushroom growth of sub-standard and slum areas in certain parts of the city. Haphazard and illegal construction of houses (both in the hills and low-lying areas), water logging, lack of proper sanitation, drainage, garbage disposal and clean drinking water, etc., are some of the problems which have plagued the citizens of Guwahati. The street food vendors, most of whom live in the sub-standard and slum areas, face these problems which are aggravated during the rainy season, when stagnant water submerges the living quarters which are also the cooking areas for many vendors.

FOOD SAFETY AND HYGIENE

Cleanliness and hygiene are of great importance in matters of food preparation and sale. In many of the tea stalls, hotels and restaurants located in the city, basic cleanliness is lacking. Street food is no exception. It is generally held by middle class people that street food is unsafe and potential health hazard. Abdul Jabber, a retired Assam Civil Service officer, aged

62 years, always discourages his grandchildren from taking street food. But Hareswar Goswami, a lecturer of a local college, aged 54 years, says that though he tries to prevent his nephews and nieces from taking street food, they always seek a chance to relish it and frequently enjoy different kinds of street foods. In this context, there is a popular children's poem by Lila Gogoi (1987:10) in his book Khara Siyalar Biya (Marriage of the Tailless Jackal), where he describes to a young boy how eating of chanachur causes stomach disorders because the ingredients like gram, etc., are of cheap variety and also cooked under unclean surroundings.

Findings of studies undertaken worldwide in the early 1980s on the sanitary aspects of street food have been summarized by Dawson and Canet (1991). The study has revealed that there is a high potential for serious health problems related to the preparation and handling of street food. Also, disposal of waste water and refuse associated with these food and roadside dust, flies and insects settling on prepared food led to the contamination of street food. The business of street food vending invariably demands a populous area and to attract customers the vendors prefer to set their food stalls by the side of the road, on the footpaths (often near open drains) and sometimes even near lavatories and garbage dumps!

> Pulin Biswas, son of a Bengali cultivator, aged 42 years, is an experienced street food seller in the Panbazar area of the city. Originally hailing from a village in the 24-Pargana district of West Bengal, he has been living in Guwahati since last 20 years. Married to a Bengali girl from Hailakandi district of Assam, he lives in a two-roomed house in the Ranibari, Panbazar area along with his three minor children. He has been selling roti-sabji, ghugni, tea, bun and pakora in a variety of locations in the city. However, the present location near a bank in Panbazar (Jasawanta Road) is by far his 'best' spot. He prefers this location to a variety of others because it is relatively safe from eviction by municipal authorities (being a side road) and from police harassment. Also, it provides a steady clientele consisting of bank employees and other shop keepers. He owns a big push cart with a license (pending renewal) on which he displays the cooked food. Pulin uses the nearby vacant areas on the roadside to prepare the food to be sold. An unused side verandah of the bank is used by Pulin and his hired help to prepare the roti, to cut and wash the vegetables for the sabji and to prepare batter for the pakora. Tea is made on the cart and the ghugni is kept warm on a stove which is placed on the cart itself. His pushcart is provided with a tin roof with no cover on its sides. This makes it open to all roadside dust and flies. Robin Das, aged 24 years, is the third son

of an Assamese cultivator. He hails from Belsor in Nalbari district (approximately 70 kms. to the north west of Guwahati). He left his village eight years ago and came to Guwahati looking for a job. After several attempts he started selling street food like bun, biscuit, cake, omelette and tea from a hired pushcart in a footpath in R.G. Baruah Road. He vended in that place for about a year but because of repeated warning from police (for blocking the foot path) he had to shift. He moved along the same road towards the State Zoo. Here, vending space was limited because there were already a large number of other food sellers. He selected a spot beyond the foot path near the entrance of the zoo. This place that he selected is just beyond the foot path, but only about 3 ft. wide. Beyond this space is an open drain about 10 ft. wide. So, like the other food vendors in the same location, he erected a bamboo platform over this drain. Then he placed the cart in the space partially between the footpath and on the platform over the drain.

Rajat Pawar (43) is a recent migrant to the city from the state of Maharashtra. He was selling roti-sabji and tea from a hired pushcart near the Panbazar water supply. After vending in that spot for a few days, he was threatened by the municipal workers who demanded a sum of Rs. 200.00 because of non possession of license. Since he was unable to manage the requisite amount within five days, he shifted his cart to another location to avoid harassment. He found a little space on one of the side roads in Panbazar. A little further (about 10 ft.) was a public urinal. On being asked about the choice of this location he replied that to avoid harassment and confiscation of property he had to shift in a hurry and did not intend to stay in that dirty area. He felt that covering of cooked food is essential and he himself has a covered cart, but the foul smell from the nearby lavatory, drain and garbage dump makes things worse. He also added that since street food is a part of the road, dust and flies are unavoidable.

Most of the food sellers try to keep the food covered. But a few of the food items like chanachur sold from trays, fruit slices and sugarcane juice are exposed to roadside dust and flies (Plate 32).

Keeping in mind the accusations of health hazard, preparation and sale of food by a few vendors were observed.

Mohan Lal (43) is a Bihari person selling chanachur in Guwahati. He lives in a one-roomed but in the Birubari area of the city along with his pet dog. His wife and four children live in his native home in Sitamarhi district of Bihar. This room is used not only for sleeping (both for him and his dog) but for cooking and eating as well. To prepare chanachur, he soaks the Bengal gram overnight in water obtained from a kaccha (mud) well where outside water seeps in. This gram is eaten raw which is salted and spiced. The quality of the ingredients used such as gram, peas and groundnuts are inferior, obtained cheaply and cooked and stored in dirty utensils. With regard to serving, the vendor uses his hands to serve which are not washed prior to serving.

Uttam Pathak (36) is a phuska vendor of Bihari origin. He lives in Fatasil-Ambari area of Guwahati city along with 33 other persons, in a shed divided into 10 compartments. Between them, they have the use of two kutcha latrines (without a septic tank) at a distance of about 15 ft. from the dwelling house. Sometimes, these latrines overflow into the small courtyard. During the rainy season, when rain water fills up the entire courtyard and enters the dwelling house, it makes conditions bad.

Use of unwashed hands, with dirty long nails, are often seen in the process of preparation of phuska, which requires kneading of the dough. Hands are also used to serve the phuska. On enquiry it was found that soap is rarely used even after releasing night soil.

After observing both preparation and sale of food, it has been seen that cleanliness is not properly maintained while handling food. Lack of consciousness regarding health and hygiene, scarcity of clean water and inadequate garbage and sewage disposal are some of the important factors which affect the 'safety' of street food. However, findings of studies to taste bacterial contamination carried out in the city of Pune in India have shown that restaurant food is no safer than street food (Kulkarni 1992). Also, findings of studies conducted in Minia in Egypt, Manikganj in Bangladesh and Iloilo in the Philippines indicate that in general "street food are as safe as or safer than food prepared in the homes of most customers" (Tinker 1987b:14). Further, cooked food consumed soon after preparation is usually safe. Contamination comes from dust and flies settling on uncovered food.

The customer survey conducted in Guwahati has revealed that in spite of the unsanitary conditions associated with street food, such food is preferred because it is cooked 'right-in-front' and served hot. This reduces chances of contamination. Also, the number of people it serves is immense.Depending upon the working population, a food vendor in a busy location in Guwahati serves over 200 people in a day. Yet very few people complain of 'food poisoning' and other stomach ailments. And if they do, these food carts would not be there the next day.

Access to Basic Infrastructure

Basic infrastructure includes the availability of safe and clean potable water, besides arrangements for the disposal of solid wastes and wastewater.

Water

Access to clean water is a major problem of the vendors and customers. Clean water for drinking, cooking, washing hands and utensils are seldom found. Table 1 shows the different sources of water used by street food vendors in Guwahati.

It is evident that tap water is commonly used (82.98%). However, tap water supplied by the Guwahati Municipal Corporation is not available throughout the day. Water is required to be stored. Further, not all parts of the city have this facility. In those localities, where tap water is not available, the vendors have to use either stored water or use water from wells (8.51%) and tube wells (5.32%) which are very limited. Rain water and/or pond water have also been found to be used by vendors (3.19%) for washing utensils.

From the baseline survey done in 2009, the position in this regard for the street food vendors of Guwahati is discussed below.

Table 7.1: Sources of Water Used by Street Food Vendors (1991)

Source	*Vendors*	
	No.	*%*
Tap	299	82.98
Well	31	8.51
Tube well	19	5.32
Pond/rain water	11	3.19

Access to Potable Water

The following table gives the various sources of potable water at the work place of the sampled street food vendors as per the survey carried out in Guwahati during April 2009.

It is seen that only 39.60% of the respondents stated that they obtained their potable water from municipal supplies. This is due to the fact that piped water supply is not available in large parts of the city, especially in the southern and western parts of the city as well as in all fringe areas of the GMC area. Over 60% of the sampled respondents were located in such places.

Table 7.2-A: Sources of Potable Water (2009)

Sl. No.	*Source of Potable Water*	*No of Responses*
1.	Water Supply (GMC etc.)	417
2.	Deep Tube Well	19
3.	Well	84
4.	Hand Pump	78
5.	Others like Purchased Water, Stream & Tank	369
6.	Not Applicable	86
	Total	**1053**

In fact, 35.04% of the sample was sourcing potable water from sources like purchased water, stream and tank. Further, 7.98% and 7.41% of the sample sourced their requirement of water from wells and hand pumps respectively.

Storage of Potable Water

Along with the source of potable water, the quality of such water is determined by the storage method used at site. In fact, the storage of potable water is an important issue in maintaining the hygienic quality of the food served to customers. Therefore, the methodology of storing water at site has been investigated during the survey. The sampled food vendors used different methods to store their requirement of water as tabulated below.

Table 7.2-B: Storage of Potable Water

Sl. No.	*Storage of Potable Water*	*No of Responses*
1.	Plastic Drum	850
2.	Tin	35
3.	Clay Pot	33
4.	Others	49
5.	Not Applicable	86
	Total	**1053**

It is seen that about 80.72% of the sampled vendors used plastic drums to store water.

(B) No of Food Vendors Using Ice

It was found that 245 street food vendors were using ice.

(C) No of Food Vendors Not Using Water in Food Preparations

It was found that 86 street food vendors responded that they did not use water at their place of sale.

Access to Toilet Facilities

(A) Toilet Facilities

The following table gives the type of toilet facilities available to the street food vendors at their place of work.

Table 7.2-C: Type of Toilet Facilities

Sl. No.	*Type of Toilet Facility*	*No of Responses*
1.	Free Toilet (with nearby establishment or residence)	147
2.	'Pay Basis' Toilet	9
3.	Open Air (including un-maintained roadside urinals / toilets)	897
	Total	**1053**

It is seen that about 85.19% of the sampled vendors used open air for toilet purpose at their place of work (including un-maintained roadside urinals / toilets).

(B) Hand Washing

Hand washing is solely done from stored water at the place of work, since none of the vendors have any source of running water near their cart or kiosk.

Waste Disposal

(A) Segregation of Wastes

There is no segregation of solid wastes into bio-degradable wastes (vegetable matter) and others like plastic, dry matter etc. In fact, in the GMC area; the householders do not practice the segregation of solid wastes.

(B) Solid Waste Disposal

The following table (Table 4-D) gives the different methods used by street food vendors for disposing solid wastes at their place of work.

Table 7.2-D: Disposal of Solid Wastes

Sl. No.	*Type of Disposal Method*	*No of Responses*
1.	Municipal Garbage Receptor (Bin / Vat)	452
2.	On the Street (Near Vending Site)	391
3.	Into Nearby Drains	112
4.	Others (Fed to Pets / Sold / Others)	98
	Total	**1053**

It is seen that 42.92% of the sample stated that they used municipal garbage receptors (dust bins / vats etc.) while 47.77% used the street or drain to dispose their solid wastes.

(C) Waste Water Disposal

Waste water is invariably disposed by either being poured into the nearby drain (if available) or onto the nearby street or ground (preferably onto porous soil nearby i.e. ground that is not covered by concrete or bitumen) – if a drain was not available.

STREET FOOD VENDORS AND CONTROL

The importance of street food as a source of income and of food for the urban populace has already been mentioned. The significance of this activity to the municipality is also immense, not only in terms of service rendered but also revenue obtained through license fees and fines. Although the role of the informal sector in providing employment opportunities to the poor is recognized, the hawkers and vendors employed in offering this essential service are the objects of antagonism and are often harassed.

Harassment

Harassment of street food vendors by police and municipal workers is common. The visits of dignitaries to the city, decision to enforce law against illegal structures, road widening or the spread of an epidemic bring stringent control upon all who sell ready-to-eat food.

Eviction

Eviction of roadside vendors to clear them of government or municipal land is conducted from time to time for which no prior notice is required (Sec. 353 of the Gauhati Municipal Corporation Act, 1969 Assam Act I of 1973). The street food sellers who are stationed near the main roads either in shop, stall or in carts are more affected in comparison to the mobile ones who can quickly move to 'safer' places before the municipal workers or the police can confront them. In the course of the field work, the present investigator had the opportunity to meet and study the displaced vendors on two occasions of eviction. The first was because of a visit by the Prime Minister to the city and the second following a routine eviction carried out from time to time by the railway authorities to clear the railway land (near Bhutnath area) of illegal structures.

Sapan Dey (38) is a Bengali wage labourer, who has recently (8 months) joined street food vending by selling tea, bun and biscuit. He is married with three children who live with him in Santipur near Bharalumukh. He is the only earning member of the family. He started a small stall near the Bharalu bridge on the side of the main road in A.T. Road. Sapan is helped by his wife who works alternately between her home and tea stall. He used to get a large number of stray and permanent customers which included policemen, shopkeepers, rickshaw pullers, school teachers and office staff. Just when his business was doing well, he was informed that he had to shift elsewhere because the main road will be cleared and cleaned for the visit of the Prime Minister. Not knowing where to go, he shifted his belongings to his rented house in the same area. Fear of eviction and destruction of property made him close his tea stall temporarily and look for other small-time job.

Ajit Kumar Das, aged 29 years, is a seller of roti-sabji and rice-based meals in the Bhutnath area of the city. This area is a very busy one, considering the fact that the public bus stand was located there for some time before it was shifted to Adabari in its permanent site. Ajit had built a temporary shed with two rooms. The first was used for the dining space with four pairs of desk and bench and the second as living and cooking space. Ajit, with the help of his brother and two hired helpers, cooks and serves meals to the bus passengers. One day at about 11 O'clock in the morning, the railway authorities accompanied by their police personnel came and partially dismantled the shop and destroyed the cooked food.

All shops and shacks,. numbering about twenty-three, were partially or totally destroyed in the process on that day. Cooked food like meals and light meals meant for bus passengers were spoilt. The vendors quickly tried to salvage some portion but the loss caused could hardly be compensated. A fortnight after the eviction, the investigator met Sri Hari Das, an Assamese vendor hailing from Darrang district (approximately 180 kms. to the north east of Guwahati, on the north bank of the river Brahmaputra) and asked him about the after effects of eviction.

Hari Das (29) used to sell meals in Bhutnath near the temporary bus stand. His brother (25) helped him in preparation and serving of meals. Two hired workers do the washing of utensils. They built a temporary bamboo structure with a polythene cover which served as the food shop. They also have a sitting and eating arrangement consisting of a plank of wood placed horizontally on four bamboo poles. This serves as the table and a smaller plank as the bench. The adjoining room served as the cooking and sleeping room. After the eviction, the temporary shed was brought down and along with it, the cooked food consisting of rice, dal, vegetables and fried fish was spoilt. Only uncooked ration could be saved. Hari has since built a smaller shack but could not afford to keep both the hired workers, so he decided to do with only one. Sale was slack immediately after eviction but picked up slowly.

Most of the evicted vendors (16) have rebuilt in the same location, while others (7) have moved to safer places in Maligaon (3), Adabari (2) and Pandu (1). The vendors had no option but to fall back on the same occupation except one vendor who had since then taken to flower selling. They feel that if they could be organized into association or union, the harassment could be largely reduced.

Overcrowding: In Guwahati, harassment of food vendors is primarily a problem of the pavement and roadside vendors. The problem arises because vendors spill over leading to overcrowding and congestion in the area. Those vendors who occupy narrow lanes and by - lanes in the busy market places have the tendency to obstruct traffic as well as movement of people. In a study conducted in Guwahati, Bora (1993:26) clearly shows that roadside parking and market area congestion are factors affecting free flow of traffic particularly in the Fancy Bazar wholesale marketing area. He also mentioned that on-the-spot vendors, narrow approach roads and present parking area of trucks and cars in Fancy Bazar riverside as other factors causing congestion. It is worth mentioning that street food vendors are not the only sellers who line both sides of the road in busy market places. There are other sellers of fish, vegetables, fruits, textiles, etc., who thrive in these areas.

Health and hygiene: Controlling of street food and quality of food sold are often justified on grounds of health. The argument is that these foods are prepared and sold under dirty conditions and hence require quality control and proper inspection. Section 227 of the Assam Municipal Act, 1956 (Assam Act XV of 1957) deals with sale, exposing for sale, etc. of food. "Any person directly or indirectly selling, exposing for selling, hawking or manufacturing, storing or possessing for sale any adulterated food shall be dealt with in accordance with the provisions of the Prevention of Food Adulteration Act, 1954 (Act 37 of 1954). For this purpose, the Board shall appoint at least one inspector for the areas under its jurisdiction". In addition to this, sections 52, 210(1) and (2) of the same act provides for the appointment of health officers - the District or Sub-divisional Medical

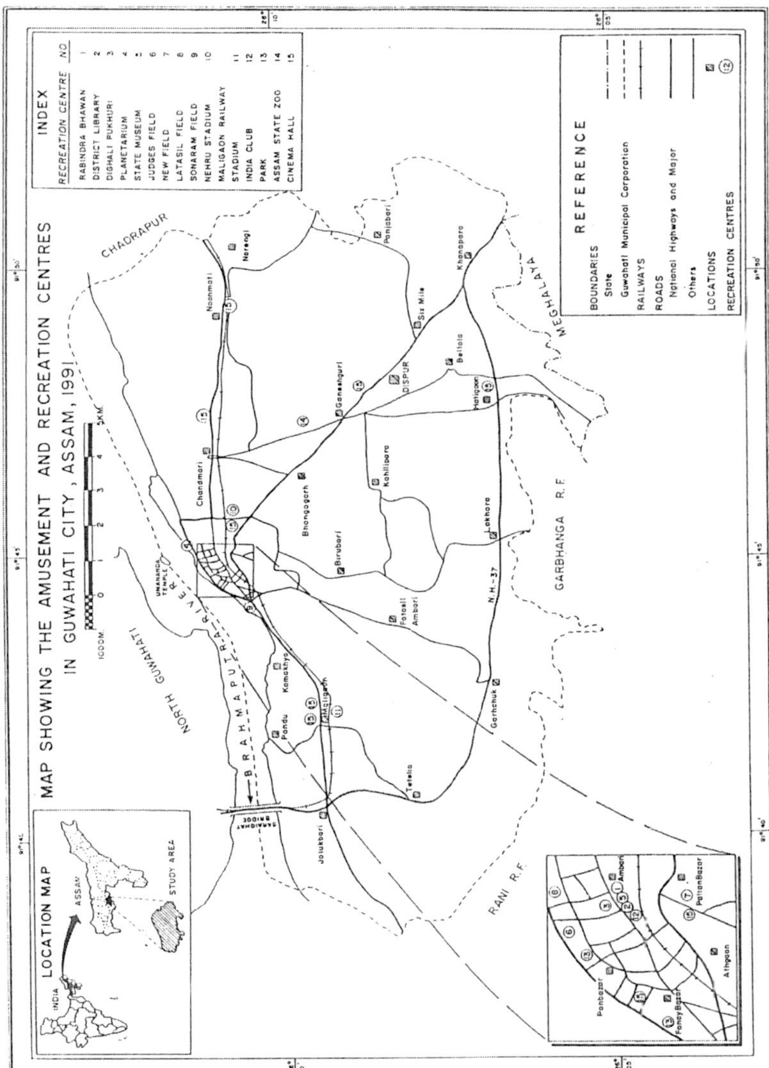
MAP SHOWING THE AMUSEMENT AND RECREATION CENTRES
IN GUWAHATI CITY, ASSAM, 1991
INDEX
RECREATION CENTRE NO
RABINDRA BHAWAN 1
DISTRICT LIBRARY 2
DIGHALI PUKHURI 3
PLANETARIUM 4
STATE MUSEUM 5
JUDGES FIELD 6
NEW FIELD 7
LATASIL FIELD 8
SONARAM FIELD 9
NEHRU STADIUM 10
MALIGAON RAILWAY STADIUM 11
INDIA CLUB 12
PARK 13
ASSAM STATE ZOO 14
CINEMA HALL 15
REFERENCE
BOUNDARIES
State
Guwahati Municipal Corporation
RAILWAYS
ROADS
National Highways and Major
Others
LOCATIONS
RECREATION CENTRES
LOCATION MAP
INDIA
ASSAM
STUDY AREA
NORTH GUWAHATI
BRAHMAPUTRA RIVER
CHADRAPUR
MEGHALAYA
GARBHANGA R.F.
RANI R.F.
SARAIGHAT BRIDGE
N.H.-37
Chandmari
Noonmati
Narengi
Panjabari
Six Mile
Khanapara
Beltola
DISPUR
Ganeshguri
Hatigaon
Kahilipara
Bhangagarh
Lakhara
Birubari
Fatasil Ambari
Garhchuk
Kamakhya
Pandu
Maligaon
Jalukbari
Tetelia
Panbazar
Fancy Bazar
Athgaon
Paltan Bazar
Amberi

Fig 3

Officer as the case may be who shall regularly but not less than twice a year inspect the different areas of the municipality and send regular reports. In the event of outbreak of any infectious disease, the municipal authority, has the power to close "... for a specified time any market, tea stalls or restaurants, hotels or lodging house within the municipality...or forbid any person to attend any such market, tea stall....". In accordance with this rule, during a jaundice epidemic in Guwahati in 19923 street food vending was regulated and controlled. All ready-to-eat food which were exposed were required to be covered. Also, sale of ice sticks, fruit slices, fruit drinks and artificially flavoured fruit drinks were prohibited till the control of the disease.

Licensing

The Guwahati Municipal Corporation tries to control street food vending by requiring licenses for trading. Under section 180(1) of The Gauhati Municipal Corporation Act, 1969 (Assam Act I of 1973), "Every person who exercises.... any of the profession, trade or calling indicated in the Fourth Schedule, shall annually take out a license before the first day of April in each year or within one month of his taking up the profession....". In Guwahati a small section (10.5%) of food vendors has licenses. These vendors include mobile sellers of chanachur, phuska, sugarcane juice pressers and a few stationary food sellers who own pushcarts. But these licenses are meant only for the pushcarts (as slow moving vehicle) and not to vend street food. The rest of the vendors have either tried to get a license but found the procedure too cumbersome or had possessed a license but did not renew subsequently. In either case the majority of street food vendors operate without any valid license. Nevertheless, all such vendors have to pay a sum of Rs. 5 per day as encroachment fee.

Any person, who without a license uses any place as specified in Sec. 229 of the Assam Municipal Act, 1956, shall be liable to a fine not exceeding one hundred rupees and to a further fine not exceeding twenty rupees every day thereafter during which the offense is continued after he has been convicted of such offense. Street food vendors often fall prey to the municipal workers because they fail to produce a license. At most times a compromise (in the form of protection money and bribes) is reached between the vendor and the workers, but sometimes the cart is seized and taken away.

> Ramen Das (27), whose heavy pushcart was seized by the municipal workers as he did not possess a license, made no move to regain his

cart. He argued that if he went to get his cart it would involve a heavy expense of not only the fine of Rs. 100.00 and the additional Rs. 20.00 per day, but would also involve bureaucratic hassles. Instead, he acquired a small table and started selling tea and confectionery items.

From the foregoing discussion, it is clear that the conditions under which food are prepared and sold, quality of the ingredients used and sanitary aspects of handling food are some of the important aspects that have to be regulated and controlled. But often it is observed that imposition of strict health codes results in bribery rather than improved hygiene. Thus, it is difficult to achieve the, desired standard without regularizing and legitimizing this activity. Further, health education and awareness on the part of both vendors and customers should be raised. Also, organizing the vendors into associations may help in voicing their grievances and in reducing harassment to a large extent.

THE STREET VENDORS (PROTECTION OF LIVELIHOOD AND REGULATION OF STREET VENDING) ACT, 2014 AND ITS IMPLEMENTATION IN GUWAHATI

For a very long time, street vending activities were considered as illegal. Although the role of the informal sector in providing employment opportunities to the poor is recognized, the hawkers and vendors employed in offering this essential service are often harassed until 1989 when the Supreme Court of India ruled that "the right to carry on trade or business mentioned in Article 19(1)(g) of the constitution, on street pavements, if properly regulated cannot be denied on the ground that the streets are meant exclusively for passing or re-passing and for no other use"(*Sodan Singh and Others vs NDMC*). But after passing this historic judgment, relief for the hawkers and vendors were not assured. The Street Vendors' (Protection of Livelihood and Regulation of Street Vending) Act, 2014 was the culmination of collective mobilisation and "bottom-up" legal activism on the part of the vendors' unions and associations especially efforts by Self Employed Women's Association (SEWA) and National Alliance of Street Vendor's India (NASVI) saw the fruition of this Act (Bhowmik 2007).

The Act aims to protect the livelihood of street vendors and provide them with a conducive environment for carrying out their business. This Act proposed to change vendors' legal status, since each municipality would be required not only to grant licenses to registered hawkers, but also to establish *Town Vending Committees* (TVC). These committees would be responsible for defining areas where street selling would be authorised

(*Hawking Zones*) and for settling conflicts between the different actors like vendors, residents, shopkeepers, municipality. This legal arrangement was therefore intended to introduce new modes of governance applicable to public space, which would include street vendors that would now enjoy new opportunities of contributing to the urban future. Despite the new law, hawking is an activity still criminalised.

In the state of Assam, the Street Vendors' (Protection of Livelihood and Regulation of Street Vending) Act, 2014 regulates street vendors in public areas and protects their rights. The Act states that all vendors are to be accommodated in vending zones and no vendors are allowed to carry out such activities in no-vending zones. But even after 5 years of its commencement, GMC is yet to implement it in full force, as reported in G Plus, an online newspaper (*GMC Fails to Implement Vending Zones even after 5 Years of Vendors' Act* by Barasha Das. January 25, 2020 15:40 hrs).

Guwahati Municipal Corporation (GMC) undertook a survey in 2015 in accordance with the provisions of the Act and showed that there were 7,183 street vendors in the city. It included 497 food vendors, 727 cloth vendors, 661 fruit vendors, 2,044 vegetable vendors, 194 fish vendors, 82 meat vendors, 1,163 paan/tamul vendors, 183 chana/puchka/bhel puri vendors and 1,631 others. However, the Assam Street Vendors' Association (ASVA) claims that there are more than 40,000 vendors in Guwahati as on date. In my survey conducted in Guwahati (GMC area) in 2009, the number of street food vendors is estimated to be about 4,500 persons in all. This excludes family members and other dependents. The above figure includes about 1,500 stationary and semi-stationary street food vendors and about 3,000 mobile food vendors. Such vendors were found to be of the following types:

(a) *Stationary food vendors*: those selling street food from a fixed location throughout the day, including those who operate from open air shops or stalls, carts which remain in the same place etc.;

(b) *Semi-stationary food vendors*: those who come to a particular fixed location only (with an ambulatory cart etc.) every day for a particular number of hours; and

(c) *Mobile food vendors*: those who shuffle from one location to another throughout the day using boxes, trays, carrying poles fitted with baskets, ambulatory carts etc.

The contradictory number of vendors reported in different surveys is a matter of concern notwithstanding the fact that vending as an activity is highly transitory. Yet, so much of variation in number reported seem unreal. The vendors listed prepared by the GMC will be accommodated in Vending Zones and if the survey shows a reduced number of vendors, then only a small number will be included and it is feared that a large section will be left out without any valid recognition.

The GMC has taken initiative to form the Town Vending Committee (TVC), a mandatory requirement under the Act. This Committee is headed by headed by the GMC commissioner with members from various sectors like NGOs, 40% members from vendors, banks and the police department. Today there are a total of 20 members with 8 members from Assam Street Vendors' Association. The activities of the TVC have been slow since meetings are not held regularly and GMC is yet to establish any vending zones in Guwahati. In the absence of all these measures, eviction is continuing causing harassment and uncertainty among street vendors. As per notification No. GDD.29/2008/Pt./277 dated 26 February 2016 in The Assam Gazette, "Every Town Vending Committee shall maintain up-to-date record of registered street vendors and street vendors to whom a certificate of vending has been issued." The record is also to be updated every three months and the returns furnished to the state government and local authorities must be uploaded on the website.

However, GMC has not yet provided any such identification or certificate. As such, there is no official record of the number of vendors or their identities.

In pursuance of decision taken by the TVC, Guwahati, in its meeting held on November, 2018, six locations were declared as vending zones under GMC, in exercise of powers conferred under section 18 (1) of the Street Vendors Act, 2014, viz. Ganeshguri (Wholesale Gali), Barbari (VIP road), Panbazar (opposite of Meghdoot Bhawan), Uzan Bazar (In front of GMC office), Fancy Bazar, (Phool Gali) and AT Road (Col. J. Ali Road).(Source: Guwahati Municipal Corporation)

Notwithstanding the fact that, the Street Vendors (Protection of Livelihood and Regulation of Street Vendors) Act, 2014 provides legal rights to the existing vendors, it restricts new entrance to the market. According to section 3 (2) of the Street Vendors Act, 2014, "The TVC shall ensure that all existing street vendors, identified in the survey, are accommodated in the vending zones subject to a norm conforming to two and half per cent of the population of the ward or zone or town or city, as the case may be".

Very recently, in an attempt to regularise the ever-increasing numbers of street vendors in Guwahati and to provide them with proper license and business amenities, the Urban Development Department has formulated a new scheme called, "The Assam Street Vendors (Protection of Livelihood and Regulation and Street Vending) Scheme 2020" on July 13 last. The new scheme is formulated under the Street Vendors (Protection of Livelihood and Regulation and Street Vending) Act, 2014 and Assam Street Vendors (Protection of Livelihood and Regulation and Street Vending) Rules, 2016. The said scheme is to come into force with immediate effect. In pursuance to the operational Guidelines of Support to Urban Street Vendors, a state-level Project Sanctioning Committee is constituted under the Chairmanship of the Principal Secretary/Secretary in Charge of Deendayal Antyodaya Yojana - National Urban Livelihoods Mission (DAY-NULM). A State Nodal Officer has been appointed under the concerned department for ensuring the implementation of the Act, Rules and the Scheme for the street vendors. The commissioner in the case of GMC and the Executive Officer of the Urban Local Body (ULB) are to be the nodal officers. The scheme mentions in detail the regulations for street vendors to provide the registered vendors with proper means to conduct regular business.

Bhowmik, S. K. (2007). "Street Vendors in Urban India: The Struggle for Recognition", in A Morales and J. Cross (Eds.), Street Entrepreneurs: People, Place and Politics, pp 92-107, New York, Routledge.

Chapter - 8

Summary and Conclusion

Street food vending is a global phenomenon. It is an ubiquitous activity not only in the Third World countries but even in the developed cities of the West. While street food vending and similar activities in the urban informal sector have been criticized by urban planners as traditional and as a reminder of underdevelopment, this study has tried to establish street food vending as an important urban service and at the same time providing employment to a large number of unskilled and uneducated people. On the basis of the data collected in the city of Guwahati,Assam, the study has tried to analyze some of the important issues, certain commonly held assumptions and the hypotheses outlined in the Chapter One.

This study outlines the genesis and spread of street food in Guwahati. Street food is relatively a new phenomenon in Guwahati which has become prevalent only during the last three to four decades. Earlier, eating of cooked food was largely confined to one's home or among people of same or similar caste status. Gradual urban development and increased cosmopolitan population, primarily due to migration of different ethnic groups, have led to relaxation of caste restrictions associated with cooking and eating of food. A new kind of food which was not confined to the domestic hearth came to be accepted.

Assamese food encompasses a variety of snacks and light meals yet, Assamese people lacked a tradition of eating out. They never patronized street food because cooking and eating were involved with ritual prohibitions and restrictions. Though many of the Assamese snacks and light meals have portability and durability and are relatively free from ritual pollution, none of these appeared as street food in the urban situation of Guwahati. As outlined in Chapter Four, none among the diverse variety of relishes, snacks, light meals, sweetmeats, fruits, juices and meals are typical Assamese food. Two of the items, chanachur and bhapa pitha have a parallel to Assamese mahkarai and tekeli mukhat diya pitha, respectively. However, the makers and sellers of these food are not Assamese but Bihari vendors. Also, these items are eaten largely by the non-Assamese people. In spite of the fact that tekeli mukhat diya pitha and boot pitha were vended in some rural markets of Assam by Assamese vendors, it is seen that none of the present street food vendors in the study sample sell these items or any other traditional snacks and light meals which have the attributes of street food.

Guwahati is not merely the largest city in north east India having a rich historical past, it has also emerged as a thriving centre of street food. It has been attracting diverse groups of people from different parts of the country as well as from within the state. In addition to a large number of migrants who have. settled here with families, there are numerous others who have come alone. They include a large number of informal sector workers, people in transferable jobs, travellers, daily commuters, etc., who are dependent on street food. It is cheap, easily available and provides snacks and wholesome meals.

It will have been noted that despite being the biggest city in the north east, Guwahati lacks basic infrastructural and urban facilities. This has also affected street food vendors and their operations. There is very limited provision of safe drinking water, drainage facility is poor, garbage disposal system is inadequate and the sewerage system can hardly sustain the city population. All these inadequacies have led to environmental degradation and make the city a very polluted locale. Street food vending under such conditions is a hazardous operation.

In Chapter Four, some popular varieties of street food have been described. It is evident that the items of food vended are not local food. These have entered Assam through diffusion along with the migration of people from different parts of India. It is these migrants who have popularized street food in Guwahati. Another significant finding is that street food comprises not only snacks and relishes but also meals.

Coming now to the street food vendors (described in Chapter Five), some important findings regarding the socio-demographic patterns and backgrounds of food vendors are highlighted here.

Street food vendors in Guwahati are middle-aged men and women hailing from different parts of Assam and the states of Bihar and West Bengal. It is a permanent activity for most of them. Educational attainment, which is an important feature of social and economic mobility, is very low among the vendors. In the study sample, more than half the vendors (55.6%) are either illiterate or barely literate and the rest have completed various levels of schooling. Out of 360 vendors, only one is a graduate and five vendors have passed the tenth standard. Under such conditions, getting job in the formal sector is difficult. Often street food vendors have been criticized by urban planners as young people waiting for jobs in the formal sector who take up this activity as a temporary work. This study reveals that street food vendors are not young but middle aged people who consider their business as a life time activity. Thus, vending in street food perhaps cannot be called as part- time or temporary activity practiced by young men while waiting for jobs in formal sector.

A look at the caste background of vendors shows that street food vendors belong to a variety of caste groups. Except for two castes, the Halwai and Moira, who are traditional sweetmeat makers, the rest do not have any background in handling or vending food as a traditional caste occupation. In the study sample, the percentages of the above mentioned caste groups are also not significant. Numerically, the 'Rajput' caste of Bihar origin predominate among the street food vendors in Guwahati. They did not have any background in cooking or selling of cooked food in their place of origin. Their dominance in street food vending in Guwahati is the result of social network, kinship, village and locality bonds leading to chain migration.

The occupational, mobility of vendors studied shows that for 9.1 per cent of vendors, selling of street food has been a part of the family business for at least two to three generations. They include Bihari chanachur and pakora sellers and some Bengali sweetmeat vendors. The rest of the vendors have been practicing agriculture and some have followed their caste occupation. Among the Assamese vendors, only one has been selling tea and snacks along with his father as a family business. The rest have no family history of selling street food.

Migration of food vendors reveals many important features. The street food vendors are rural migrants hailing from Bihar, West Bengal and different parts of Assam. A considerable proportion of them have lived in the city for more than two years and out of them 52.31 per cent have completed 10 years of stay in Guwahati. Some of them have sold the same items and in the same location over a long period of time. One of the main causes of migration is rural poverty. Other causes are pull of the city, maladjustment in family, etc. Many of the migrant vendors possess agricultural land (including 159 permanent migrants and 31 seasonal migrants) but it is not enough to sustain the family. During planting and harvesting seasons some of the vendors visit their natal home and assist in agricultural activities.

The family structures of the vendors studied reveals that nuclear family predominates. The families of the vendors who live in the study area, are nuclear in type. While families living in the villages are by and large variation of nuclear family or of the joint family type. The average size of the vendors' family is 6.75.

The street food vendors of Guwahati have been divided into stationary and mobile based on their nature of vending. Though numerically the mobile vendors predominate, truly mobile vendors are rare. Only those selling sweetmeats and snacks like laddu, chips, fruit slices, etc. are truly mobile. The rest have one or two regular points from where they vend.

The study of food vending locations in Guwahati reveal that they are found in all areas of the city. High concentrations of street food vendors are found near market places, recreation centers, schools, offices, hospitals, railway and bus stations, etc. A look at the distribution of different types of food vendors show a concentration in the main commercial areas of Fancy bazar, Pan bazar, Athgaon and Paltan bazar.

In the street food trade, as described in Chapter Six, vendors do not keep written records. Therefore, by estimating daily costs and observing daily sale, the return on this trade has been calculated. The average income has been found to be Rs. 50.00 per day. However, income varies within this activity. Male vendors make more income than female vendors because a female vendor has to attend to the family and perform household tasks.

Women in the street food trade reveals that though they constitute only 3.9 per cent of the total study sample, their income is vital. Out of 14 women vendors, six are sole supporters, six works with their husbands and two run street food enterprises to supplement their husband's income.

In Guwahati, the enterprises are generally of one-person type usually run by the vendor himself with additional support from family members and hired workers. The other type consists of two-person enterprises run by husband and wife or partnership between brothers, friends or other relatives. There is only one enterprise run by three persons.

Regarding division of labour in a couple-run enterprise, the preparation of food done at home was the wife's task but, at the place of sale, she assumes a secondary role. It has been observed that in some of the enterprises, woman makes the beginning, when she becomes successful, she is joined by her husband and later, on attaining further success, the wife. is withdrawn from the enterprise because it becomes a matter of prestige for a successful man to engage his wife in the trade.

Expansion of street food trade is an indication of growth. Certain important conclusions can be drawn. Vendors would like to expand but because of financial constraints, and harassment by police and municipal authorities very few vendors actually do so. This study has shown that instead of investing in the trade, profit is utilized in other directions. But vendors belonging to the higher income group have expanded. Such expansion is usually by increasing inventory and by employing additional labour.

The street food activity relatively requires very little skill which can be learnt as apprentice or at home. People without any skill for other jobs find it convenient to start this activity easily and with minimum investment. Thus, street food vending, which is characterized by ease of entry, minimum investment, small size of operation, etc., draws a large section of people towards this activity.

The discussion on municipal control over street food has shown that though it provides employment to many and constitutes an essential service in the fast developing city of Guwahati, the vendors are also persecuted and there is considerable antipathy towards them. The argument is that street food vendors make and sell edibles under dirty conditions, block roads and is a symbol of urban blight to be removed. But this argument cannot be the sole reason for the government and municipal authorities to drive away food vendors. Little do the authorities realize the growing significance of street food vending to the economy and society at large. In a country like India, where unemployment is rampant, street food vending plays an important role in providing self employment to a large section of people. But this important service has not been legitimized. The street food vendors of Guwahati are not given trade licenses to vend. The vendors with pushcarts are merely given licenses for slow moving vehicles.

Street food has emerged in the study area largely as a result of migration of diverse groups of people due to urbanization and industrialization, relaxation of caste restrictions associated with cooking and eating because of increased cosmopolitanism and the need to eat from out-of-home sources in an urban environment cheaply and quickly. Today street food has become an indispensable part of the city life.

The Marxists and liberal economists had predicted that street food vending would disappear in due course of time. Instead, it has only flourished over the years. Keeping in mind its importance as a source of self employment and in rendering a valuable service, pursuing a more sympathetic policy by the relevant administrative agencies of the government will lead to a healthy growth of this activity. Following a policy of harassment and indifference will hardly eliminate the problems of congestion or dirty environment. What is required is awareness of the problem and concerted effort to try and create a support system which will legitimize the street food sector.

It is suggested that concerned authorities should recognize street food vending as a required urban amenity and not as a nuisance to be done away with. The nuisance perception arises from the fact that the vendors create congestion on the road, traffic hazard as well as health and pollution problems. Hence, the popular argument that they have no business to be on the street and that they must be shifted from the pavements. Keeping in view the genuine service that street food vendors provide to commuters and humble workers in the city on the one hand and the commonly recognized problems of urban life that they create on the other, the following suggestions are offered which could help this informal yet vital service sector and also mitigate the problems.

(i) Legitimized space should be provided to the street food vendors in the high vending concentration areas but a little away from the main roads, preferably in a side road where customers can reach them. This will help eliminate congestion in the area at large and reduce pollution.

(ii) The food vendors should be registered for a specified time period and a fee charged from them for the space. This money should be utilized directly in the maintenance of the space allotted. Basic facilities like drinking water, garbage disposal, lighting, etc. should be provided.

(iii) There is a need for creation of "food parks" in select recreation centers where cleanliness and hygiene are strictly maintained.

(iv) Vendors should be made aware of the importance of hygiene and at all stages of handling food. Regular inspections should be conducted from time to time.

In conclusion, this study calls upon all concerned to legitimize this vital service and support it through proper planning so as to make street food vending healthy, convenient and desirable.

References

ACHAYA, K.T. 1994. Indian Food. A Historical Companion. Delhi : Oxford University Press.

ALI, A.N.M. IRSHAD. 1974. Social relations among the Assamese Muslims in Rural and Urban situations. Guwahati : Gauhati University. (Unpublished Ph.D. Thesis).

ASSAM MUNICIPAL ACT 1956. (Assam Act XV of 1957).

BAPAT, MEERA. 1990. Informal Sector Street Food Vendors : A Study in Pune (India). Pune : Centre of Studies in Social Sciences.

- 1992. Street Food Vending in Pune. Pune : Centre of Studies in Social Sciences.

BARTH, G.A. AND MEI-JEAN KUO. 1984. Crossing the Gap Between Microeconomic Activities and Small-Scale Food Catering Establishments. Washington, DC : Equity Policy Centre.

BHAGABATI, A.C. 1992. Social Formation in North East India. Bulletin of the Department of Anthropology, Gauhati University. VI : 9-27.

BHAGABATI, A.C., M. DAS AND A.N.M. IRSHAD ALI. 1986. Evaluation Through

Holistic Study of the Pilot Project on Computer Literacy and Studies in Schools (CLASS) Programme (Guwahati Project). Department of Anthropology, Gauhati University. (Mimeographed).

BHATTACHARYYA, N.N. 1990. Changing Face of Gauhati City. Souvenir, Fourteenth Annual Conference of North East India Geographical Society. Department of Geography, Gauhati University. pp. 5-9.

BHOWMIK, S. K. (2007). "Street Vendors in Urban India: The Struggle for Recognition", in A Morales and J. Cross (Eds.), Street Entrepreneurs: People, Place and Politics, pp 92-107, New York, Routledge.

BORA, P.K. 1993. Delay and Congestion studies of Road traffic on some selected roads of Guwahati. Guwa4hati: Assam Science Society.

BORA, S. 1997. Treatment of Drinking Water. The Sunday Sentinel. April 20.

CANTLIE, AUDREY. 1984. The Assamese. London : Curzon Press Ltd.

CHAPMAN, B. 1984. Street foods in Indonesia Vendors in the Urban Food Supply. Chevy Chase, MD : Equity Policy Centre.

CHOUDHURY, N.C. 1990. Piping Haute from Bengal. The Sunday Review. The Times of India. February 18.

CHOUDHURY, N.K. 1981. Census of India, 1981, Town Directory, Series-3, Assam, Part X-A. Guwahati : Director of Census Operation, Assam.

CHOUDHURY, P.C. 1959. The History and Civilization of the People of Assam to the 12th Century A.D. Guwahati : Department of Historical and Antiquarian Studies in Assam, University of Gauhati.

CRAWLEY, E.A. 1927 [1902]. The Mystic Rose : A Study of Primitive Marriage and of Primitive Thought in its Bearing on Marriage. Rev. and enl. by Theodore Besterman. London:Gale.

DAS, BARASHA. 20202. "GMC Fails to Implement Vending Zones even after 5 Years of Vendors' Act" G Plus January 25. 15:40 hrs).

DAWSON, R.J. AND C. CANET. 1991. International activities in street foods. Food Control. 2(3):135-139.

DEWAN, V.K. 1988. North-Eastern Region Municipal Acts and Rules (2nd Edition). Allahabad : Orient Law House.

DIRECTORATE OF ECONOMICS AND STATISTICS. 1993. Statistical Hand Book of Assam. Gauhati : Government of Assam.

DOUGLAS, M. 1972. Deciphering a Meal. Daedalus. 101(1):61-81.

DUBOIS, ABBE J.A. 1906. Hindu Manners : Customs and Ceremonies. Tr. by H.K. Beauchamp. Oxford : Clarendon Press.

DUMONT, D. 1970. Homo Hierarchicus : The Caste System and its Implications. Tr. by M. Sainsbury. Chicago : The University of Chicago Press.

FORTES, M. AND SONIA L. FORTES. 1936. Food in the Domestic Economy of the Tallensi. Africa. 9:237-76.

GOGOI, L. 1987 .Khara Siyalar Biya.Tinsukia, Assam: Mitra Agency & Co.

GOODY, JACK. 1982. Cooking, Cuisine and Class : A Study in Comparative Sociology. Cambridge : Cambridge University Press.

GUTHE, C.E. AND M. MEAD. 1945. Manual for the Study of Food Habits. Report of the Committee on Food Habits. Bulletin of the National Research Council 3. Washington National Academy of Sciences.

HUTTON, J.H. 1951. Caste in India. Bombay : Oxford University Press.

INTERNATIONAL LABOUR OFFICE (ILO). 1972. Employment, Incomes and Equality : A Strategy for Increasing Productive Employment in Kenya. Geneva: ILO.

KALRA, J. 1992. The Romance of Food. Sunday Magazine, The Telegraph, April 26.

KATONA-APTE, J. 1975. "Dietary Aspects of Acculturation : Meals, Feasts and Fasts in a Minority Community in South Asia" in Gastronomy. The Anthropology of food and food habits. Edited by M.L. Arnott. pp. 315-26. The Hague : Mouton.

KHARE, R.S. 1976. The Hindu Hearth and Home. New Delhi : Vikas Publishing House, Pvt. Ltd.

- 1976. Culture and Reality : Essays on the Hindu System of Managing Foods. Simla: Indian Institute of Advanced Studies.

KHARE, R.S. 1992. The Eternal Food. Gastronomic Ideas and Experiences of Hindus and Buddhist. New York : State University of New York.

KUJORE, 0.0., T.O. PEARCE AND V. AINA AGBOH. 1986. Effects of Road Clearance on the Street Foods Enterprise in Ile-Ife. Ile-Ife, Nigeria : University of Ife.

KULKARNI, A.P. 1992. Food quality control and processing. Eating on the run. Food Laboratory News, 8(2):10-13.

LEVI-STRAUSS, C. 1963. Structural Anthropology. Tr. C. Jacobson. New York : Basic Books. 1965. Le triangle culinaire. L 'Arc. 26:19-29.

LOZA, SARAH. 1985. Street Foods and Beverages in Minia City. Chevy Chase, MD: Equity Policy Centre.

MAJUMDAR, G.P. 1935. Food : Man's Indebtedness to Plants. Indian Culture. 1,3:407-420.

MARRIOTT, McKIM. 1955. Village India : Studies in the Little Community. Chicago: University of Chicago Press.

McSWINEY, J. 1912. Census of India, 1911, Assam. Calcutta : III,1.

MINTZ, S. 1979. Time, Sugar and Sweetness. Marxist Perspective. 2:56-73.

NEOG, M. 1966. Purani Asamiya Samaj Aru Sanskriti. Guwahati : New Book Stall.

SHARMA, S. 1994. Fresh Food Joints. *Saturday Fare. The Sentinel.* August 3.

SINHA, ANIL KISHORE. 1986. Anthropology of Sweetmeat : Its Tradition and Diffusion with Special Reference to Bihar and West Bengal. Ranchi : Ranchi University. (Unpublished Ph.D. Thesis).

SMITH, ROBERTSON. 1889. The Religion of the Semites. New York : D. Appleton and Co.

SRINIVAS, M.N. 1952. Religion and Society Among the Coorgs of South India. Oxford : Oxford University Press.

SZANTON, C. AND N. SIRISAMBHAND. 1986. Thailand's Street Vending : The Urban Informal Sector and Traditional Fast Foods. Chevy Chase, M.D. : Equity Policy Centre.

THE GAUHATI MUNICIPAL CORPORATION ACT, 1969. (Assam Act I of 1973).

TINKER, IRENE. 1987. Street Foods : Testing Assumptions About Informal Sector Activities by Women and Men. Current Sociology. 35, 3:1-73. 1987.

- The Case for Legalizing Street Foods. Ceres 119, 20/5:26-31. 1994. The Urban Street Food Trade : Regional Variations of Women's Involvement. pp. 1-26. (Manuscript).

OWENS, N. AND N. HUSSAIN. 1984. Street Foods in Bangladesh. Chevy Chase, MD : Equity Policy Centre.

PATOWARY, A. 1997. Guwahati a city of Tantalus ? The Assam Tribune. April 27.

PIDDINGTON, RALPH. 1957. An Introduction to Social Anthropology. London : Oliver and Boyd. Vols. I and II.

PILLAI, R.S.N. AND V. BAGAVATHI. 1984. Statistics. Theory and Practice. N. Delhi : S. Chand & Co. Ltd.

POSNER, JILL. 1984. Street Foods in Senegal. Chevy Chase, MD : Equity Policy Centre.

RADCLIFFE-BROWN, A.R. 1948. The Andaman Islanders. Glencoe, Ill. : Free Press.

RAO, M.S.A. 1974. The Migration to the City. Yojana. 18, 20:7-13. Editor. 1986. Studies in Migration Internal and International Migration in India.

RICHARDS,AUDREY. 1932. Hunger and Work in a Savage Tribe. London : Greenwood.

- 1939. Land, Labour and Diet in Northern Rhodesia. London : Oxford University Press.

ROMATET, E. 1983. Calcutta's Informal Sector : Theory and Reality. Economic and Political Weekly. 18, 50:2115-2128.

TINKER, IRENE. 1997. Street Foods : Urban Food and Employment in Developing Countries. New York : Oxford University Press.

TRIPATHY, S.N. AND SOUDAMINI DAS. 1991. Informal Women Labour in India. N. Delhi : Discovery Publishing House.

Appendices

Appendix - I

Basic Information Schedule

1. (a) Name
   (b) Sex :
   (c) Age :
   (d) Educational standard.
      (i) Illiterate
      (ii) Barely literate
      (iii) Upto
   (e) Marital status
      (i) Married
      (ii) Unmarried
      (iii) Widowed
      (iv) Divorced/Separated
2. (a) Religion :
   (b) Sect :
   (c) Caste :
   (d) Sub caste :
3. (a) Mother tongue :
   (b) Community :
   (c) Place of birth :
      (i) State :
      (ii) District :
      (iii) Police station :
      (iv) Village :
4. How many years ago, at what age he/she left the village:
      (a) Place lived since then with occupations.
      (b) Present place of residence :
      (c) Place of last residence :

	Place No. of Years	*Occupation*	*Reason for leaving*
(i)			
(ii)			
(iii)			
(iv)			
(v)			

5. Living status in Guwahati :
   (a) Alone :
   (b) With relatives (specify) :
   (c) If with family then :

Members & relationship to head	*Age*	*Sex*	*Marital Status*	*Occupation*	
				Primary	*Secondary*

   (d) Type of residence in Guwahati :
      (i) Rented
      (ii) Own
      (iii) Others (specify)
6. Street food vending.
   (a) For how many years he/she has been in the present trade:
   (b) Members of the family helping in this trade : specify :
   (c) No. of workers :
      (i) Family members alone :
      (ii) Family members and hired workers : specify :
      (iii) Hired workers only :
      (iv) Any minor workers :
   (d) Any other occupation(s) of the informant
      (i) Which is primary :

7. (a) Type of establishment :
    - (i) Push cart
    - (ii) Balance poles
    - (iii) Baskets
    - (iv) Shops
    - (v) Stalls
    - (vi) Others (specify)

   (b) Type of food sold :

   (c) Food considered as :
    - (i) Breakfast :
    - (ii) Lunch :
    - (iii) Snack :
    - (iv) Dinner :

   (d) Area of operation :
    - (i) Stationary :
    - (ii) Mobile :

   (e) Place of work :
    - (i) Name :
    - (ii) Distance to area of operation :
    - (iii) Transport :

   (f) Hours of work :
    - (i) By actual worker :
    - (ii) By other members :
    - (iii) Leisure activity outside the normal hours of work

   (g) Utensils made of :
    - (i) Cooking :
    - (ii) Serving :

   (h) Cooking arrangement :
    - (i) Type :
    - (ii) Since when in use :
    - (iii) Fuel :

   (i) Income & expenditure :
    - (i) Daily :
    - (ii) Monthly :

Comments of the investigator:

Appendix - II

Customer Survey Schedule

(a) Location :

(b) Type of vendor and food sold :

(c) Date of collection :

Identification marker of customers (collected at the time of buying/others)

1. Sex and approx. age :
2. Educational status :
3. Marital status :
4. Locality :
   (i) Home address :
   (ii) Present place of residence :
5. Occupation :
6. Place of work :
7. (i) Religion and Sect :
   (ii) Caste :
   (iii) Community :
   (iv) Mother tongue :
8. (a) Which place outside home do you eat at ?
   (b) How often ?
   (c) Types of street food consumed ?
9. Which types of street food do you prefer and why ?
10. Approx. amount spent on street food.
11. What is the importance of street food in your daily life ?
12. Give your opinion about street food (in details) : outlining: hygiene, price, convenience, time-saver, variety of food etc.
13. Any suggestions regarding the improvement of street food enterprise.

Appendix - III(a)

Unhygienic Condition in City's Hotels and Restaurants

By A Staff Reporter

GUWAHATI, Aug 25—It seems that the people in this B-21 city are quite ignorant about the need for maintaining hygienic condition in the tea stalls, restaurants, fast food corners etc., while these shops also do not bother about maintaining any hygienic standard. In most of the tea stalls, fast food corners and restaurants of the city, food items meant for human consumption are kept in open space and they become the happy hunting ground for flies. Most shops do not keep their utensils clean and some of them even go to the extent of cooking foodstuff in open areas near roads. The Gauhati Municipal Corpora-tion has framed a good number of rules in a bid to maintain the hygienic condition in the stalls, restaurants, etcf. In the !city but these rules are not followed properly. One such GMC rule says that every place where 'articles intended for human consumption are kept for the purpose of sale shall always be kept in a clean sanitary 'condition and shall be provided with sufficient means for effectual drainage and an adequate supply of filtered water. But unfortunately most of the tea stalls clO not provide filtered water to the customers and they get their water from the nearby tube wells or roadside water taps. Some of the tea stalls store their water in dirty drums which may help ' increase the medical bill of the consumers. The rules chalked out by the GMC also provide no person shall keep for sale any article which Is unwholesome or unfit for human consumption, no person shall keep for sale or sell any article intended for human consumption over or alongside any open drain or which 30 ft of sites where, dustbin, public latrines or public urinals have already , been placed, every person dealing in any articles intended for human consumption shall adopt measures to avoid deterioration of such articles and shall ensure that no dust or smoke enters the place where storage or service of food stuff is done and in no case the oven or chula shall be placed in front of the premises, etc. But unfortunately. none of these rules is strictly followed by most of the shops in the city. In most places, the kitchen or open chulas are placed near the busy roads of the city and exposed to dust while some shops have their chulas near the open drains, It is ' not that t only 'the temporary shops or tea stalls do not follow this rule. Some of the oldest ' restaurants also maintain habit of placing their chulas In front of the restaurant premises. Most of the •restaurants near the ASTC bus stand and the Railway ' Station in Paltanbazar place 'their chulas near the main road and they also keep their foodstuff in open space. ' '!' When asked to comment' on these aspects, the GMC Commissioner, Sri B N Bora said that they had imposed fines on many of these restaurants but the follow up actions could not be taken properly.'•He also agreed that most restaurants and tea stalls of the city did not follow the rules laid down by the GMC but 'it is not easy for us' to demolish these restaurants as we do not get any cooperation from the local people'.

The rules laid down by the GMC "also provide that the shop owners shall ensure that furnaces and the kitchens are of such a nature that could prevent any nuisance from smoke and that in no ease shall roadside furnaces or ovens be allowed. But the kitchens of most of the restaurants are so made that they have become a nuisance to the residents of the area. The GMC has also chalked out , many other rules like providing proper ventilation, keeping the utensils clean proper storage of uncooked food, how foodstuff should be served, etc. But the GMC bothers little to check whether all these rules are followed or not 'and as a result, very few of the restaurants bother to follow the rules. Some restaurants also have the habit of throwing all the rubbish in the nearest available ' open space or on the, roads. This restaurant owners allege that they are forced to do that as the GMC has failed to provide adequate)dustbins; But The GMC authorities on the other hand claim that the people of the city, do it want to walk a few steps to dump their rubbish in the dustbins and they Just, dump all their rubbish on the roads. They also, claim that in some cases the dustbins provided by the GMC were stolen by some people who sell irons or tins. The GMC Commissioner, Sri' Bora claimed that all these have happened because; the people are ignorant of the need for maintaining hygienic condition. The restaurants will be forced to maintain hygienic condition if the, people force them to do so, he added.

Appendix - III(b)

Unhygienic Food Joints Mushrooming in City

By Bijay Sankar Bora

GUWAHATI, May 25— Using money Guwahatians are buying diseases thanks to our penchant for eating out in unhygienic roadside eating joints which are mushrooming day by day in the city.

As a result cases of gastroenteric and hepatitis diseases in the city are on the upswing.

Most of the popular fast-food joints in the city are found to be placed in unhygienic surroundings not to speak of numerous cooked-food vendors on wheels.

Some of these eateries even do not have enough space not only to accommodate customers but even the food items. It is disturbingly common to see flies feasting over uncovered dishes while customers sit in chairs near or ever the pavement without giving a damn to air-borne dust particles and toxic emission from ever increasing number of vehicles in the city.

Knowing fully well that in such injurious environment the food they are eating will have toxic particles deposited on them, the eaters are compelled to frequent such eating places in absence of alternative.

If one is very conservative about purity of the food one takes, then he or she has to either forget eating out in the city or to go for the posh restaurants which in turn puts extra pressure on the wallet.

It is quite but natural that anyone with an eye for fast buck will go for food joints business to cash in on the tremendous demand for those in the city which has turned out to be the hub centre of all activities in the region. But the responsibility lies with concerned agencies including Guwahati Municipal Corporation, Health Department to ensure prevalence of hygienic condition in eating outlets.

As things stand as of now, the agencies are not equipped with proper mechanism to check unabated growth of such eateries some of which display exotic names to attract customers. While public health is in danger, the concerned agencies are busy shifting responsibility.

While it is a well-known fact that the city people are reeling under acute drinking water scarcity with only 35 per cent of the population having access to piped water, the enforcing agencies are turning a blind eye as to where such eateries collect water from. It is a common sight in the city especially in morning hours that numerous. watermen carrying water from suspect sources to city restaurants.

Health Department is content with once in a blue moon checking of food and water samples from the eating outlets despite a top official of the Department admitting that unhygienic eating places are posing threat to spread gastroenteric and hepatitis diseases.

By his own admission the GMC Commissioner, Sri RN Sharma said that most of the cater-wheelers seen in the city did not have the necessary license for trading in food items. These are simply equipped with a license to ply handcarts.

Unless the public and the enforcing agencies come together to stop the growth of such unhygienic eating outlets, Guwahatl will hit the headlines as one of the most gastroenteric and hepatitis prone city in the country.

The Assam Tribune. 26 May. 1997

Glossary

Ahin	:	September-October
Ahu	:	Summer paddy
Akhoi	:	Parched rice
Ambubashi	:	A period in the month of Ahar (June-July). It is believed that the earth attains menstruation during this period
Anaras	:	Pineapple
Anda	:	Egg
Anja	:	Curry
Arhar	:	A variety of pulse
Bara	:	A variety of rice
Besan	:	Chick pea flour
Bhaji	:	Is a fried item, usually of vegetables
Bhakat	:	A devotee
Bhapa pitha	:	Steamed rice cake similar to the Tekeli Mukhat Diya Pitha
Bhat	:	Boiled Rice
Bhatura	:	Deep fried, leavened bread
Bhelpuri	:	Mixture of crushed crisps, puffed rice, sweet and sour chutney and fragrant coriander leaves
Bihu	:	The national festival of Assam. There are three Bihus - Bohag Bihu or Rongali Bihu, Kati Bihu or Kongali Bihu and Magh Bihu or Bhogali Bihu
Boot	:	Bengal gram, also a variety of pulse
Boot pitha	:	A sweet prepared by mixing parched Bengal gram with Jaggery
Brahmin	:	superior most caste of the Hindus
Bundiya-bhujia	:	A sweet salty mixture
Chadar	:	A long piece of cloth used by Assamese women to cover the upper part of the body
Chana	:	Chick peas kabuli chana
Chanachur	:	Is a mixture prepared from gram, groundnuts, puffed rice, etc.
Chapati	:	Dry, roasted unleavened bread
Char	:	Riverine Tracts

Chaat	:	spicy, tangy, mashed potatoes
Chaut	:	March-April
Chhana	:	Indian cottage cheese. Acid-precipitated 'milk solids
Chunga pitha	:	rice cake prepared in the cylindrical section of green bamboo
Chuwa	:	Ritual pollution
Cira	:	Flat rice
Dab	:	tender coconut
Dal	:	A lentil soup preparation
Dala	:	A circular bamboo basket from which Phuska Is vended
Dambaru	:	A small hand-drum
Doi	:	Curd
Dosa	:	Rice and lentil pancake
Durga puja	:	Autumn festival to propitiate Mother Goddess Durga
Gamocha	:	An Assamese towel, woven in handloom
Ganne ka ras	:	Sugarcane juice
Ghee	:	clarified butter
Ghila pitha	:	Circular rice cake Ghugni/choley Chick pea curry
Gur	:	Jaggery
Handi	:	A large clay pot hat weekly market
Hawa Mithai	:	Air-filled sweet
Hira	:	A scheduled caste of Assam whose traditional occupation is pottery making by hands without the use of potter's wheel
Hurum	:	A kind of puffed rice
Idd	:	Muslim religious festival
Jajmani	:	Patron-client relations
Jalpan	:	Light meals
Jeth	:	May-June
Jhal	:	Spicy and hot
Jhalmuri	:	Spicy puffed rice
Jilebi	:	Coiled, tubular, fried pastry soaked in sugar syrup
Jira pani	:	Sour, spicy liquid
Jogi	:	A caste of Assam whose traditional occupation is silkworm rearing
Joha	:	A variety of rice
Jola	:	Pungent
Juhal	:	Tea room
Kacca	:	Food cooked in water
Kaibarta	:	A scheduled caste of Assam whose traditional occupation is fishing Kalai A variety of pulse
Kalita	:	A respectable agricultural caste of Assam
Karigar	:	Helper or apprentice

Kecha pithaguri	:	Uncooked rice flour
Khar	:	alkaline
Khira	:	Cucumber
Khoa	:	Thickened milk, almost solid
Khurara	:	A mixture of flour, gram flour, clarified butter and sugar
Khurma	:	Sweet snack of wheat flour
Komal chaul	:	Softened rice
Kulfi	:	A kind of Ice Crème
Kutcha	:	Earthen
Laddu	:	Sweet balls, also known as Laru in Assamese language
Magu	:	Green gram
Mahkarai	:	Mixture of parched lentil, Bengal gram, rice and sesame
Maida	:	Refined wheat flour
Makkai	:	Corn
Malbhog	:	A variety of rice
Malpua	:	A sweet snack of wheat and sugar syrup
Masur	:	A kind of pulse
Matar	:	Meal peas pulse
Mati mah	:	A kind of pulse
Mihidana	:	Very fine sweet fritters
Mumphali	:	Groundnuts, it is also known as badam in Assamese language
Mung	:	A variety of pulse
Muri	:	Puffed rice
Narial	:	Coconut
Narikal laru	:	Coconut balls
Nimki	:	Salted, triangular dough crisps
Pakghar	:	Kitchen, where rice and other side items are cooked
Pakka	:	Food cooked in ghee
Pakora	:	Fritters, known by different names bara, vada, pakauri, pakoda, bor, phulori, etc.
Pankha mithai	:	Fan-shaped sweet
Papita	:	Papaya
Paratha	:	Pan-fried wheat circlet
Payas	:	Rice cooked in sweetened milk
Phuska	:	Dough puffs filled with a sour, peppery liquid. It is also known as gol gappa or pani puri
Pitha	:	Rice cake
Pithaguri	:	Rice flour which has been roasted
Poharis	:	Women vendors mostly belonging to low castes
Poka mithoi	:	Sweet ball prepared with uncooked rice flour and jaggery
Prasad	:	Ritual offering

Pucca	:	Concrete
Pulao	:	Meat-rice dish
Puri	:	Deep fried puffed out wheat meal circles. It is known as luci in Assam and West Bengal
Rajasik	:	Conducive to passion
Randhanighar	:	Kitchen, where rice and other side items are cooked

PLATES

Plate 1: Different ingredients of *chanachur.*

Plate 2: A *chana* vendor selling from a box.

Plate 3: A vendor with a covered pushcart selling *chanachur*.

Plate 4: *Chanachur* vendors outside a girls' college.

Plate 5: School children buying relishes.

Plate 6: *Phuskas* stacked on a *dala*.

Plate 7: A *phuska* vendor selling from a mobile pushcart near a children's park.

Plate 8: Customers crowding around a *phuska* vendor.

Plate 9: A *bhelpuri* seller.

Plate 10: A seasonal migrant vendor roasting groundnuts.

Plate 11: Woman vendor roasting groundnuts in a street corner.

Plate 12: A groundnut and popcorn seller.

Plate 13: Woman vendor roasting corn over a makeshift fireplace.

Plate 14: A *chat* seller colourfully displays his fare.

Plate 15: College students and office goers having chowmein.

Plate 16: A vendor selling *roti-sabji*, egg, patties, etc., in addition to *pulao*.

Plate 17: Sweetmeats and snacks being sold during *Idd.*

Plate 18: Vendor selling *hawa mithai.*

Plate 19: Young boy selling chips in front of a mosque during *Idd.*

Plate 20: A *kulfi* seller.

Plate 21: Cool cucumber slices served on a hot afternoon.

Plate 22: A sugarcane crushing machine parked along a main road.

Plate 23: A tender coconut seller near the Deputy Commissioner's office.

Plate 24: A seller of coloured drinks waiting for customers.

Plate 25: Two brothers busy preparing *parathas* near the T emporary Capital Complex at Dispur.

Plate 26: Fish, pork and egg being prepared in a shack near a sweeper's colony.

Plate 27: A young boy engaged in street food business.

Plate 28: Vendors doing brisk business during the Guwahati Book Fair

Plate 29: A case of vendor expanding his business.

Plate 30: One-roomed shack in a slum used for both living and cooking purposes.

Plate 31: Vendors cooking in the open along a dirty road.

Plate 32: Uncovered *chanachur* and cucumber slices being served.

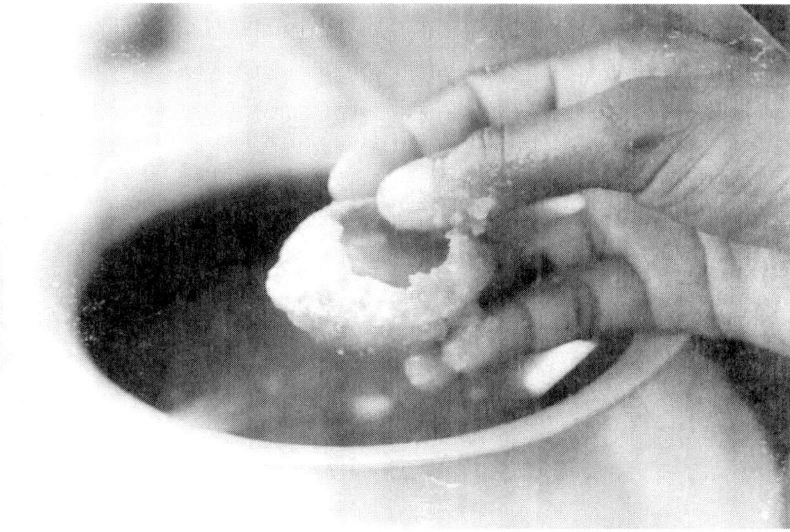

Plate 33: Hand being used tu serve *Phuska.*

Plate 34: Vendors stationed along the footpath near Deputy Commissioner's office.

Plate 35: Vendors moving into the main road near a children's park